BUSINESS BASICS Series

Focuses on a variety of situations involved in business and provides opportunities to improve learners' communication skills in the workplace.

BUSINESS BASICS 2

CARROT HOUSE

CARROT HOUSE
P.O.Box #2924, St. Marys, Ontario, Canada

Business Basics 2
ⓒ Carrot House

All rights reserved. No part of this publication may be reproduced,
stored in a retrieval system, or transmitted in any form or by any means
without the prior permission in writing of Carrot House

Printed September 2019

Author : Carrot Language Lab

ISBN 978-89-6732-115-4

Printed and distributed in Korea
9th F, 488 Gangnam St, Gangnam-gu, Seoul, 06120, Korea

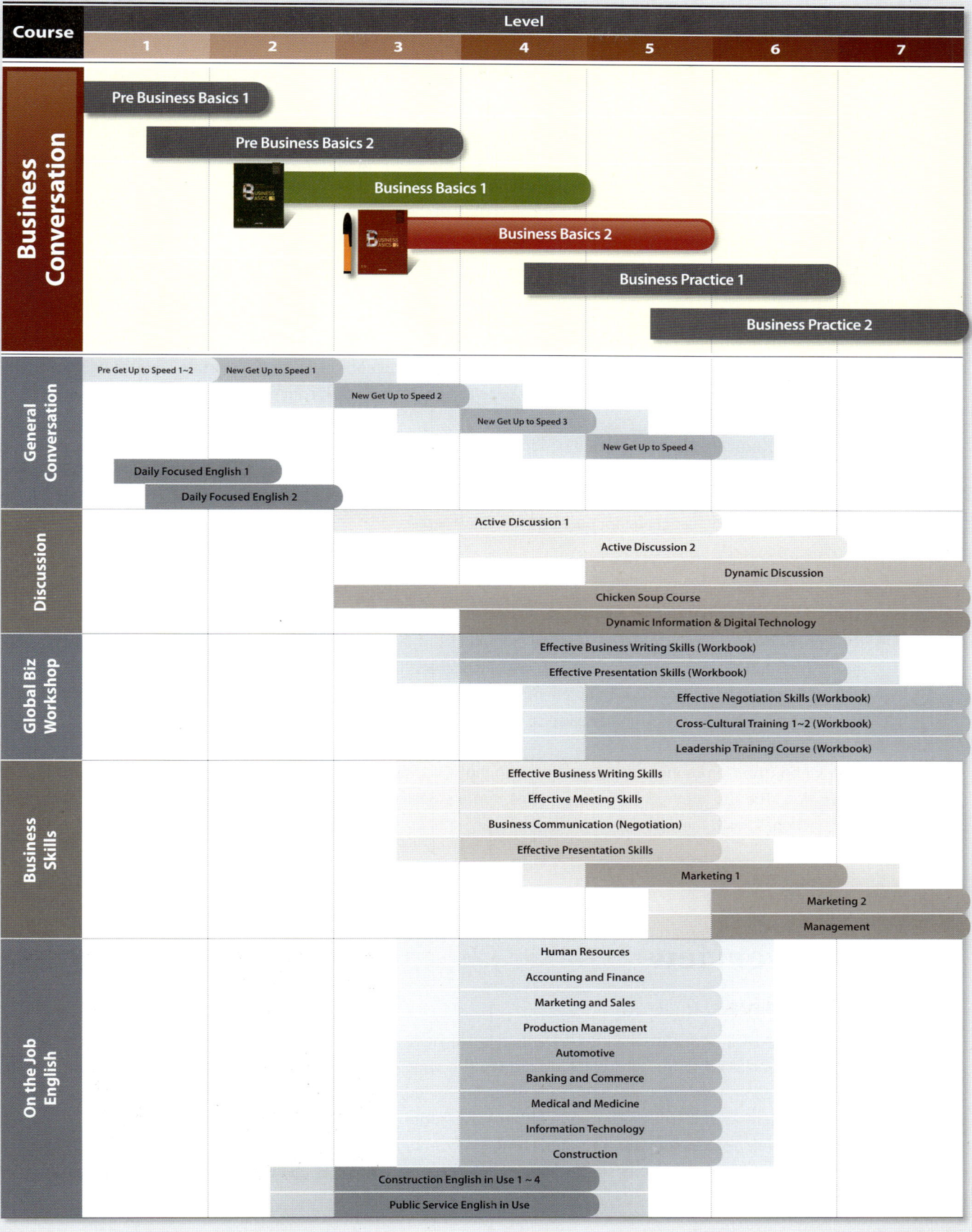

BUSINESS BASICS 2

Introduction

Carrot House Methodology — Andragogical Approach & Productive English

The teaching of children (pedagogy) and adult learning (andragogy) are distinctively different. Pedagogy is akin to training and encourages convergent thinking and rote learning. It is compulsory, centered on the teacher and the imparting of information with minimal control by the learner. Andragogy, by contrast, is about education as freedom. It encourages divergent thinking and active learning. It is voluntary, learner oriented and opens up vistas for continuing learning. Adults need to feel independent and in control of their learning. Therefore, Carrot House curriculum is based on andragogy and is designed to encourage learners' participation and engagement by providing more task-based activities and opportunities to frequently interact in the classroom.

People want to achieve communicative competence when they learn other languages. English education in EFL environments has been rather focused on the receptive skills of English—listening and reading—which simply increases learners' knowledge about a language, not the competence of using it. If people are well equipped with productive skills—speaking and writing—they will be competent in English communication.

This is why Carrot House curriculum is designed to enhance learners' productive skills throughout the course. This andragogical approach of the Carrot House Curriculum, which focuses on productive English, will enable learners to achieve communication skills necessary for global competence. Carrot House's teaching philosophy and curriculum combine to provide a "Language for Success" for all learners.

Communicative Language Learning (CLL)

This communicative interaction, the essential component of language acquisition, does not occur in a typical, non-meaningful, fun-oriented conversation with native speakers. It occurs in a negotiated interaction through which a well-trained teacher provides the comprehensible input that is appropriate to the learners. The learners, at the same time, actively utilize the opportunities given to them by the teachers.

To this end, the Communicative Language Learning (CLL) method is employed in the field of Foreign Language Acquisition. The CLL method provides activities that are geared toward using language pragmatically, authentically and functionally with the intention of achieving meaningful purposes.

Course Overview

I. Objectives

BUSINESS BASICS Series is designed to enhance learners' communication skills in the workplace by providing a wide range of situations involved in business. Each series is targeted at intermediate level learners. Through constant classroom interactions, learners can improve their productivity proficiency to achieve success in international transactional situations.

II. How to use Business Basics 2

Lesson Composition
The book consists of 16 lessons (4 units) based on topics of great interest to everyone involved in business. The composition of each lesson is as below.

Learning Objectives
Set clear goals to acknowledge target learning of each lesson

- Go over the learning objectives with learners to understand the learning focus
- Review the objectives at the end of each lesson to reinforce each point

Situational Dialogue
Understand the mission of each business character and role play to practice English speaking in business situations. Help learners improve their comprehension skills and utilize useful expressions.

- Have learners answer questions about the characters to check their understanding of the mission and business situation
- Pair up class to practice the dialogue and compare with their own work
- Give feedback on each learner's role play
- Allow learners to answer the discussion comprehension questions

Getting Started
Stimulate learners' thinking and put them at ease in an English speaking environment through situation-related questions and an introduction to language tones

- Open the class with discussions questions and encourage learners to brainstorm answers together
- Allow learners to differentiate between formal and informal expressions

Fun Facts
Presents interesting facts for learners to reflect upon and express their own opinions

- Learners can reflect on information and discuss whether it comes as a surprise or expected fact
- To be used flexibly

BUSINESS BASICS 2

Language Focus
Reinforce useful business expressions and patterns through substitution drills. Learners will practice how to use the essential expressions within their business lives

- Have learners study the expression and learn how to apply it in various situations
- Have learners review expression and key patterns by creating their own sentences

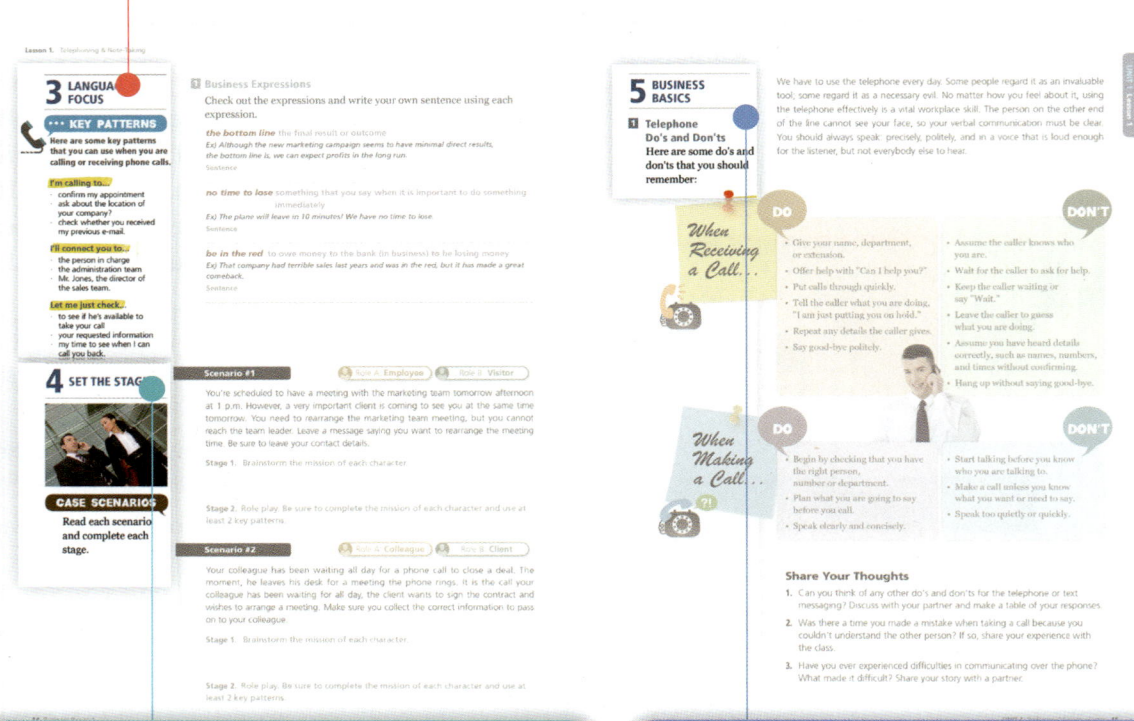

Set the Stage
Reinforce learners' response skills in various business situations through case scenarios activities. This will enable learners to apply the thematic situations and the skills of global business communication

- Pair up class to review each scenario
- Have learners follow each stage to create dialogue and role play using the background information provided
- Give feedback on each learner's role play
- Each lesson has 2 case scenarios to review

Business Basics
Expand learners' ability to develop essential business skills, such as making presentations, taking part in meetings, telephoning, and using English in social situations. Learners will learn business manners or etiquette through the medium of English.

- Have learners read the background information and complete the task as a pair or as group work
- Encourage learners to 'share their thoughts' by sharing their personal experience, ideas and opinions in more depth

Numbers & Facts

Provides learners' with additional information in the medium of tables and charts regarding the Business Basics theme

- Allow learners time to read and understand the information
- Review learners understanding of the given data through presentations and questions

Cultural Notes

Provides learners with background information on the cultural etiquettes and behaviors

- Learners can review the information and compare with similarities and differences of their own culture
- To be used flexibly

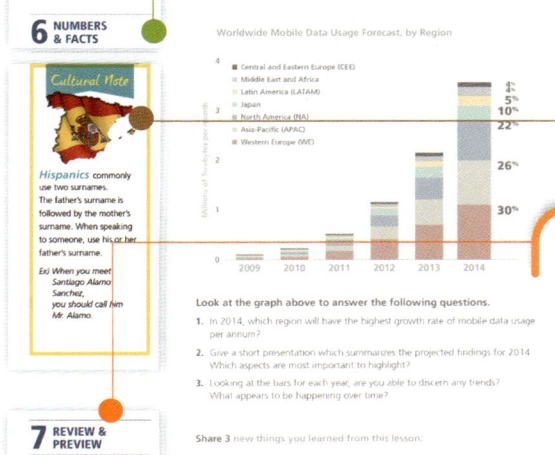

Review & Preview

Recall and review material learned each lesson as well as preview the following lesson through discussion topics

- Go through review questions with learners to follow up on learning objectives mentioned at the start of the lesson
- Discuss preview questions leading up to the following lesson topic

2 Case Studies

The Case Studies are based on realistic business situations and problems. They will encourage students to develop communication skills and problem solving skills by giving them opportunities to practice in realistic business situations.

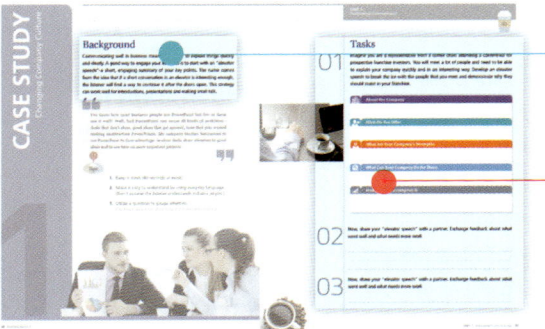

Background Information

Have learners read and understand background information about the company and situation

Task

Have learners complete an activity that encourages them to think about the problem in each case study and how the company or individual can address the problem

- Pair up or form groups to talk about the problem
- Ask learners to think about how the problem should be dealt with

Presentation Encourage learners to present their solutions as they would in real business situations

- Allow individual or group work to present solutions, the logic behind the solutions, and their expected outcomes

Contents — BUSINESS BASICS 2

Unit 1. Professional Communicator

Lesson Title	Learning Objectives	Key Patterns	Business Basics
Lesson 01 **Telephoning & Note-Taking** → page 10	• to make/receive phone calls properly • to practice leaving and taking messages	• I'm calling to… • I'll connect you to… • Let me just check…	Telephone Do's and Don'ts
Lesson 02 **Communication & Culture** → page 15	• to recognize and understand diversity and culturally determined differences in communication practices • to discuss cultural differences in body language, gestures, and communication styles	• What I mean is… • I'm sorry I didn't… • You seem to…	Nonverbal Communication; Cultural interpretations
Lesson 03 **Presentation Know-how** → page 20	• to use skills for effective presentations • to discuss verbal and physical delivery aspects of presentations	• We can begin by looking at… • As a final point, I'd like to… • What you're asking is…	Effective Presentation Skills
Lesson 04 **Situational Communication Strategies** → page 25	• to apply different communicational strategies in various situations; such as showing sympathy, confronting problems, and giving compliments	• I'm sorry to hear about… • You look … today • I want to talk to you about…	Communication Strategies; Thomas-Kilmann Conflict Mode Instrument
CASE STUDY → page 30	**Powerful communication – Elevator Speeches** Task: To promote your company to prospective investors and buyers through communication techniques		

Unit 2. Winning Negotiator

Lesson Title	Learning Objectives	Key Patterns	Business Basics
Lesson 05 **Proposal & Negotiation** → page 32	• to enhance knowledge and skills related to business negotiate and articulate your position • to make business proposals and counter-proposals	• You might be interested in… • I'm thinking of… • What do you think about…	Effective Negotiation Skills
Lesson 06 **Tackling Problems** → page 37	• to discuss solutions to business problems and consider the consequences of possible course of action • to find compromises in conflict solutions	• I suppose we can… • It would save time to… • This could lead to…	Hidden Traps in Decision-Making
Lesson 07 **International Negotiations** → page 42	• to handle cultural differences during the negotiating process • to recognize different negotiation styles	• I understand that… • I'd be interested to hear about… • Can we agree on…	International Negotiation; Need to know
Lesson 08 **Taking a Position** → page 47	• to state/clarify your position and persuade others to support your side • to close a negotiation	• Let me recap… • That's a good point, but… • I can go along with…	Closing the Deal; Getting it done
CASE STUDY → page 52	**Cross-cultural Negotiations - Strategies and Preparations** Task: To strategize methods for successful cross-cultural negotiations by understanding cultural factors		

Unit 3. Positive Interaction

Lesson Title	Learning Objectives	Key Patterns	Business Basics
Lesson 09 **Using Humor** → page 54	• to ease a tense situation through witty comments • to recognize different types of witty comments and show humor	• Better late than never, but better never late! • dot your i's and cross your t's • You can't have your cake and eat it, too.	Witty Comments and Comedic Skills
Lesson 10 **Turning the Table** → page 59	• to use strategies to turn the business situation to your advantages • to persuade others with evidence and supporting detail	• I see no choice but to... • According to..., it seems that... • I'd be willing to comply if you...	Turning the Table : Skill Set
Lesson 11 **Invitations** → page 64	• to cordially invite people out for meals • to make reservations at a restaurant	• When's a good time to... • Do you prefer... or... • What would you recommend for...	Invitation Styles
Lesson 12 **Maintaining Positive Relationships** → page 69	• to use various methods to compliment others • to recognize different ways to maintain and establish positive relationships in the workplace	• You look... today • What's your secret for... • I think you have great...	Relationship Skills
CASE STUDY → page 74	**Maintaining Employee Morale - Programs and Incentives** Task: To create solutions and brainstorm practical ideas to raise company morale and encourage colleague bonding		

Unit 4. Cultural Diversity

Lesson Title	Learning Objectives	Key Patterns	Business Basics
Lesson 13 **Cultural Mistakes** → page 76	• to discuss the importance of cultural awareness and common cultural mistakes people make • to discuss major cultural differences between Eastern and Western cultures	• You can call me... • I didn't know about... • In..., we...	Cultural Mistakes; Preventing culture shock
Lesson 14 **Cross-cultural Business Etiquette** → page 81	• to recognize different cross-cultural values • to explore global business manner, etiquette, and protocol	• I consider... to be the most important... • ... is considered rude. • I'm sorry; I didn't catch...	Cultural Mistakes; Etiquette points
Lesson 15 **Expatriate Employees** → page 86	• to recognize cultural challenges expatriates face abroad • to discuss ways to ease the transition into a new culture	• I suggest that... • The most challenging thing about... was... • I have to tell you that...	Culturally Diverse Workforce
Lesson 16 **Body Language Across Cultures** → page 91	• to review gestures and nonverbal communication of other countries • to understand the concept of personal space in different cultures and discuss how it is incorporated in business	• I didn't intend to... • I don't think it's such a great idea to... • You should avoid ...ing	Cultures and Body Language
CASE STUDY → page 96	**Globalization and Business - Cultural Awareness** Task: To debate on the importance of cultural awareness to be successful on the global market		

LESSON 01

UNIT 1. PROFESSIONAL COMMUNICATOR

Telephoning & Note-Taking

Overview

- [ ] Getting Started
- [ ] Situational Dialogue
- [ ] Language Focus
- [ ] Set the Stage
- [ ] Business Basics
- [ ] Numbers and Facts

[Learning Objectives] Upon completion of this lesson, you will be able to…
- make/receive phone calls properly
- practice leaving and taking messages

1 GETTING STARTED

1 Warm up

Let's open the floor. What are your opinions?

01.
What is some basic information you should give to the other person when making a call?

02.
How many calls do you receive on average each day? What are your calls usually about?

03.
Why do you think note-taking is important? What are some effective note-taking skills that you would recommend?

2 Formal vs. Informal

Write the correct phrases in the formal or informal column of the table according to the tone.

a. Drink, anyone?
b. Sorry.
c. I'll call you later.
d. Bye.
e. Is Monica there?
f. I do beg your pardon.
g. How are you?
h. Hi there.
i. How is it going?
j. How do you do?
k. I will telephone you after six o'clock.
l. Where are the toilets?
m. Would you mind repeating that for me?
n. Excuse me?
o. It has been a pleasure to meet you.
p. May I offer any of you another drink?
q. Could you please direct me to the restroom?
r. Could you put me through to Ms. Jones, please?

Function	Formal	Informal
Greeting		
Asking after health		
Offering		
Asking for someone		
Asking for repetition		
Apologizing		
Asking for directions		
Making arrangements		
Saying good-bye		

2 SITUATIONAL DIALOGUE

1 Before reading the dialogue, use the information given below to answer the following questions.

Mr. Higgs — Brian Higgs, the assistant manager of S&G Company
MISSION: To effectively and efficiently manage calls and messages for his boss, Jack.

Mr. Andes — Johnson Andes from the advertising team
To confirm with Jack the schedule of a conference call they have prearranged.

1. Look at the characters and describe the situation.
2. What is the relationship between the characters?
3. What do you think will happen next?

2 Practice the dialogue and answer the comprehension questions.

Taking a Call

Mr. Higgs: Good morning. This is Brian Higgs, the assistant manager of S&G. Can I help you?

Mr. Andes: Oh, good morning. Is Jack in?

Mr. Higgs: No, I am afraid he's out of the office today. May I ask who's calling?

Mr. Andes: Yes, this is Johnson Andes from Wilmington. I wonder if I could leave a message?

Mr. Higgs: Certainly, Mr. Andes.

Mr. Andes: Could you ask Jack to call me regarding the conference call we've arranged for Wednesday the 30th? It's quite urgent.

Mr. Higgs: Regarding the conference call on the 30th? Right. I'll let him know. Does he have your number?

Mr. Andes: Actually, I'll give you my mobile number. It's easier. It's 0446 6565 7877.

Mr. Higgs: That's 0446 6565 7877.

Mr. Andes: Correct. Thanks for your help.

Questions

1. What is an example of good telephone etiquette you can see in the dialogue?
2. Your boss is writing an important report and doesn't want to be disturbed. However, someone is demanding to speak with your boss saying it is urgent. What do you do?
3. Imagine you are Mr. Higgs taking notes for the call. What would you write in your notepad?

FUN FACTS
Did you know?

❶ Alexander Graham Bell (US), the inventor of the telephone, thought the phone should be answered by saying "Ahoy" or "Hoy Hoy".

❷ An average person makes about 1,140 telephone calls each year.

Lesson 1. Telephoning & Note-Taking

3 LANGUAGE FOCUS

••• KEY PATTERNS

Here are some key patterns that you can use when you are calling or receiving phone calls.

I'm calling to...
- confirm my appointment.
- ask about the location of your company.
- check whether you received my previous e-mail.

I'll connect you to...
- the person in charge.
- the administration team.
- Mr. Jones, the director of the sales team.

Let me just check...
- to see if he's available to take your call.
- your requested information.
- my time to see when I can call you back.

4 SET THE STAGE

CASE SCENARIOS

Read each scenario and complete each stage.

1 Business Expressions

Read the expressions and write your own sentence using each expression.

the bottom line the final result or outcome
Ex) Although the new marketing campaign seems to have minimal direct results, the bottom line is, we can expect profits in the long run.
Sentence

no time to lose something that you say when it is important to do something immediately
Ex) The plane will leave in 10 minutes! We have no time to lose.
Sentence

be in the red to owe money to the bank (in business) to be losing money
Ex) That company had terrible sales last years and was in the red, but it has made a great comeback.
Sentence

Scenario #1

Role A: **Employee**   Role B: **Visitor**

You're scheduled to have a meeting with the marketing team tomorrow afternoon at 1 p.m. However, a very important client is coming to see you at the same time tomorrow. You need to rearrange the marketing team meeting, but you cannot reach the team leader. Leave a message saying you want to rearrange the meeting time. Be sure to leave your contact details.

Stage 1. Brainstorm the mission of each character.

Stage 2. Role play.
Be sure to complete the mission of each character and use at least 2 key patterns.

Scenario #2

Role A: **Colleague**   Role B: **Client**

Your colleague has been waiting all day for a phone call to close a deal. The moment, he leaves his desk for a meeting the phone rings. It is the call your colleague has been waiting for all day, the client wants to sign the contract and wishes to arrange a meeting. Make sure you collect the correct information to pass on to your colleague.

Stage 1. Brainstorm the mission of each character.

Stage 2. Role play.
Be sure to complete the mission of each character and use at least 2 key patterns.

5 BUSINESS BASICS

1 Telephone Do's and Don'ts

Here are some do's and don'ts that you should remember:

We have to use the telephone every day. Some people regard it as an invaluable tool; some regard it as a necessary evil. No matter how you feel about it, using the telephone effectively is a vital workplace skill. The person on the other end of the line cannot see your face, so your verbal communication must be clear. You should always speak: precisely, politely, and in a voice that is loud enough for the listener, but not everybody else to hear.

When Receiving a Call...

DO
- Give your name, department, or extension.
- Offer help with "Can I help you?"
- Put calls through quickly.
- Tell the caller what you are doing, "I am just putting you on hold."
- Repeat any details the caller gives.
- Say good-bye politely.

DON'T
- Assume the caller knows who you are.
- Wait for the caller to ask for help.
- Keep the caller waiting or say "Wait."
- Leave the caller to guess what you are doing.
- Assume you have heard details correctly, such as names, numbers, and times without confirming.
- Hang up without saying good-bye.

When Making a Call...

DO
- Begin by checking that you have the right person, number or department.
- Plan what you are going to say before you call.
- Speak clearly and concisely.

DON'T
- Start talking before you know who you are talking to.
- Make a call unless you know what you want or need to say.
- Speak too quietly or quickly.

Share Your Thoughts

1. Can you think of any other do's and don'ts for the telephone or text messaging? Discuss with your partner and make a table of your responses.

2. Was there a time you made a mistake when taking a call because you couldn't understand the other person? If so, share your experience with the class.

3. Have you ever experienced difficulties in communicating over the phone? What made it difficult? Share your story with a partner.

Lesson 1. Telephoning & Note-Taking

6 NUMBERS & FACTS

Cultural Note

Hispanics commonly use two surnames. The father's surname is followed by the mother's surname. When speaking to someone, use his or her father's surname.

Ex) When you meet Santiago Alamo Sanchez, you should call him Mr. Alamo.

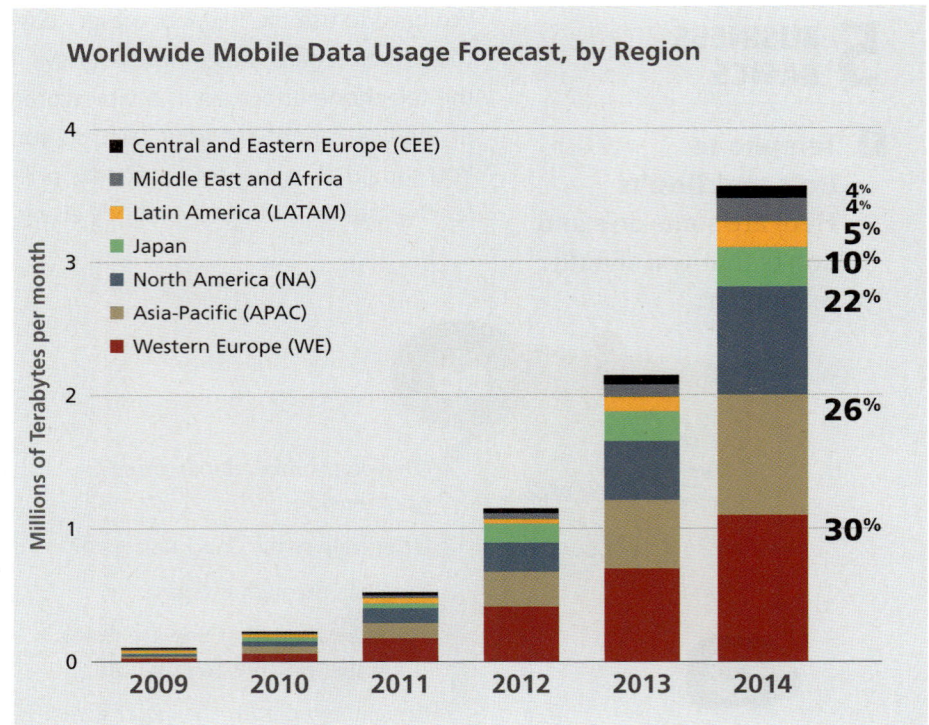

Look at the graph above to answer the following questions.

1. In 2014, which region will have the highest growth rate of mobile data usage per annum?

2. Give a short presentation which summarizes the projected findings for 2014. Which aspects are most important to highlight?

3. Looking at the bars for each year, are you able to discern any trends? What appears to be happening over time?

7 REVIEW & PREVIEW

Share 3 new things you learned from this lesson:

1.

2.

3.

Sneak Peek

1. What are some communication cultural difference between the Western culture and the Eastern culture?

2. What is nonverbal communication? When do you use nonverbal communication?

14 Business Basics 2

LESSON 02

UNIT 1. PROFESSIONAL COMMUNICATOR

Communication & Culture

Overview

- [ ] Getting Started
- [ ] Situational Dialogue
- [ ] Language Focus
- [ ] Set the Stage
- [ ] Business Basics
- [ ] Numbers and Facts

[Learning Objectives] Upon completion of this lesson, you will be able to…
- recognize and understand diversity and culturally determined differences in communication practices
- discuss cultural differences in body language, gestures, and communication styles

1 GETTING STARTED

1 Warm up

Let's open the floor. What are your opinions?

01.
What are some cultural differences that you have observed when interacting with foreigners? Explain.

02.
Why do you think it is important to be aware of cultural differences when interacting with people from other cultures? Support your opinion with details.

03.
How would you explain your country's communication style to a foreign visitor? Are there any types of body language or gestures that they should be aware of?

2 Formal vs. Informal

Write the correct phrases in the formal or informal column of the table according to the tone.

a. What do you mean?
b. Great work!
c. Ms. Jones, Mr. Smith.
d. Thanks.
e. I got it.
f. No, thank you. I'm fine.
g. Sorry.
h. I'm okay.
i. What do you think?
j. I'd like to apologize for my mistake.
k. I would like to hear your thoughts on the issue.
l. Ms. Adams, I'd like to introduce you to Mr. Gregg.
m. I'm sorry, but could you explain that again?
n. Please excuse me for a minute.
o. I understand your point.
p. I'll be back in a minute.
q. Thank you for your kind words.
r. You did an excellent job on the last project.

Function	Formal	Informal
Asking for clarification		
Apologizing		
Offering a compliment		
Accepting a compliment		
Introducing others		
Refusing a drink		
Excusing yourself from a conversation		
Expressing understanding		
Asking for an opinion		

UNIT 1. Professional Communicator 15

2 SITUATIONAL DIALOGUE

1 Before reading the dialogue, use the information given below to answer the following questions.

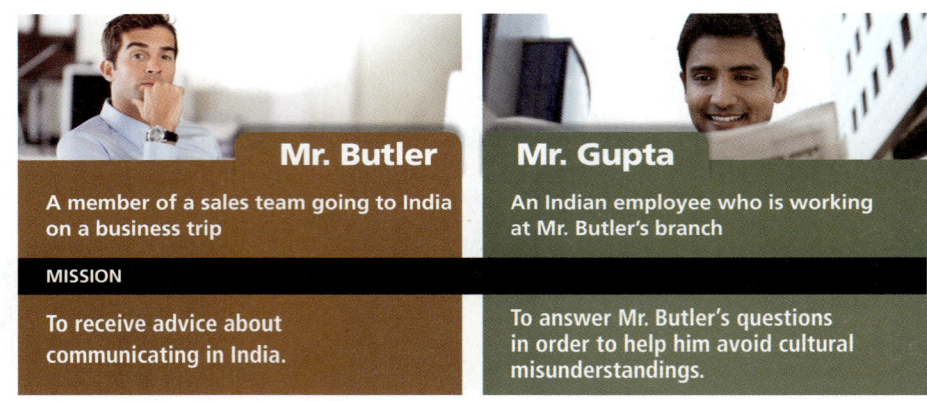

Mr. Butler
A member of a sales team going to India on a business trip

MISSION
To receive advice about communicating in India.

Mr. Gupta
An Indian employee who is working at Mr. Butler's branch

To answer Mr. Butler's questions in order to help him avoid cultural misunderstandings.

1. Look at the characters and describe the situation.
2. What is the relationship between the characters?
3. What do you think will happen next?

2 Practice the dialogue and answer the comprehension questions.

Expat: New Country, New Style of Communication

Mr. Butler: Hello, Mr. Gupta. How are you doing today?

Mr. Gupta: I'm fine. How about you? Are you ready for your business trip to India?

Mr. Butler: More or less. I was just wondering if I could ask your advice on a few things. What I mean is, I want to prepare myself for cultural differences I might encounter in India. Do you have any advice?

Mr. Gupta: Yes, of course. I'm sorry I didn't offer to help sooner. What would you like to know?

Mr. Butler: Well, how should I greet people?

Mr. Gupta: You could simply shake hands, or you could say "Namaste" while putting your hands together. Doing that would show that you are trying to understand the culture.

Mr. Butler: That's helpful. Is there any body language I should be aware of?

Mr. Gupta: Be careful when waving hello. You seem to use that gesture a lot. Some Indians might confuse the Western side-to-side hand wave as "no" or "go away."

Mr. Butler: I never knew that. This has really been helpful.

Mr. Gupta: It was my pleasure. Please let me know if you think of any more questions before you leave.

Questions

1. What are some other questions you would ask if you were Mr. Butler?
2. Are there any gestures in your country that have different meanings in other cultures?
3. What are some differences that you have observed when traveling abroad?

3 LANGUAGE FOCUS

••• KEY PATTERNS

Here are some key patterns that you can use when discussing cross-cultural communication and cultural differences.

What I mean is...
- how are you doing today?
- we are impressed with the quality of your work.
- we would be happy to reschedule the meeting.

I'm sorry I didn't...
- offer you a drink.
- explain that more clearly.
- understand what you just said.

You seem to...
- be very knowledgeable about the culture.
- have many interesting things to say.
- be upset about something.

4 SET THE STAGE

CASE SCENARIOS

Read each scenario and complete each stage.

1 Business Expressions

Read the expressions and write your own sentence using each expression.

on the borderline barely acceptable in quality
Ex) Bill's job performance is really on the borderline. He's lucky that he hasn't gotten fired yet.
Sentence _____

all ears prepared to listen attentively
Ex) What happened in the meeting? I'm all ears.
Sentence _____

off the hook to be no longer in difficulty or trouble
Ex) I can't believe Jack finished the project by himself. I guess we're off the hook.
Sentence _____

Scenario #1

Role A: Employee who is preparing to go on a business trip to Canada
Role B: Co-worker who has experience working abroad

You are an employee of an international company at the headquarters in Tokyo, Japan. Next week, you will leave for a month-long business trip to Canada. Your supervisor has asked you to speak with one of your more experienced co-worker about cultural differences that you might encounter in order to improve your communication strategies. Ask your co-worker questions and compare experiences that you have had interacting with Westerners.

Stage 1. Brainstorm the mission of each character.

Stage 2. Role play.
Be sure to complete the mission of each character and use at least 2 key patterns.

Scenario #2

Visiting representative from the Head Office in New York
Manager of the Beijing branch

You have been sent to a regional branch of your company to evaluate their ability to communicate with foreign clients. You need to give feedback to the branch's manager about the communication strategies they use with Western customers. Try to explain the issue in a tactful way by illustrating differences between the two cultures.

Stage 1. Brainstorm the mission of each character.

Stage 2. Role play.
Be sure to complete the mission of each character and use at least 2 key patterns.

Lesson 2. Communication & Culture

5 BUSINESS BASICS

FUN FACTS

Did you know?

❶ Did you know that Hartsfield-Jackson Atlanta International Airport (USA) is the world's busiest? Each year, 95.5 million passengers pass through and 930,000 takeoffs and landings occur.

❷ Did you know that as a plane ascends and the pressurizing of the air cabin numbs about a third of our taste buds? As a result, food does not taste as appealing.

Rhetoric refers to humans' terrific ability to use words, phrases, and the total the power of language to persuade other humans. Humans, however, are also very physically attuned. We respond to what we see in another person's face, body, mannerisms, gestures, and overall behavior. Nonverbal (without the use of language) communication is a significant component of how two people view each other.

Gesture	Eastern Interpretation	Western Interpretation	My Interpretation
Direct eye-contact	Assertive and rude	Attentive and honest	
Smiling at strangers and saying hello	Usually a bit awkward since the two people have never formally met	Signals outgoingness, friendliness, and a democratic mind	
Emphatic hand gestures	Usually a bit too dramatic and considered "emotional"	Acceptable and could even show the energy and enthusiasm of the speaker	
Head bowing	Very reverent and polite; a hallmark of the culture	A bit subservient and more appropriate for religious contexts or not at all	
People of the same gender holding hands	A sign of deep friendship and bonding	Very strange for heterosexuals and uncommonly seen	

Share Your Thoughts

1. Fill in the chart above with your interpretation for each gesture. How do you feel about each one?

2. Which foreign gestures do you find most interesting? Which foreign gestures most irritate you? Why?

3. How would you respond to a foreign person in your country doing an incorrect or inappropriate gesture?

6 NUMBERS & FACTS

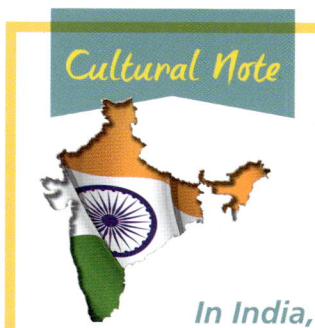

Cultural Note

In India, touching another person even in a slight way like stepping on his or her toes is considered very offensive. One way to apologize is to tap the other person, usually on the shoulder, and then to touch your own forehead immediately with the same hand.

Look at the image above to answer the following questions.

1. What percentage of travelers had medical issues while traveling? How many were hospitalized?

2. Traveling is not risk free. Use the chart to give a short presentation about travelers' top concerns. What is your top concern when traveling?

3. Using the two sides of the information table, how justified do you think travelers' worries are? Do you think travelers over-worry, or do you think that their fears are rational?

7 REVIEW & PREVIEW

Share 3 new things you learned from this lesson:

1.

2.

3.

 **Sneak Peek**

1. How do you feel before a giving a presentation? Do you have any strategies for getting ready?

2. What's the worst thing that you could do during a presentation?

LESSON 03

UNIT 1. PROFESSIONAL COMMUNICATOR

Presentation Know-how

Overview

- [ ] Getting Started
- [ ] Situational Dialogue
- [ ] Language Focus
- [ ] Set the Stage
- [ ] Business Basics
- [ ] Numbers and Facts

[Learning Objectives] Upon completion of this lesson, you will be able to...
- use skills for effective presentations
- discuss verbal and physical delivery aspects of presentations

1 GETTING STARTED

1 Warm up

Let's open the floor. What are your opinions?

01.
What do you consider to be the characteristics of a good presentation? Explain.

02.
Do you give many presentations for your job? How do you prepare?

03.
What tips would you give someone who has never given a presentation before? What should he or she be aware of?

2 Formal vs. Informal

Write the correct phrases in the formal or informal column of the table according to the tone.

a. Sales have gone up 10% in the last few weeks.
b. Check out this chart.
c. Let's start now.
d. Yes, Ms. Marks?
e. Hi, everyone.
f. Any questions?
g. I think we're done here.
h. Our research shows a 2% increase in sales of the product.
i. Does anyone have anything to ask?
j. Do you have something to add, Mr. Dale?
k. And with that, I will conclude my presentation.
l. Good morning, ladies and gentlemen.
m. I would like to turn the floor over to Mr. James.
n. We will begin by discussing new business.
o. This graph shows a good improvement.
p. As you can see in the graph, sales have increased steadily over the past year.
q. Could everyone please refer to diagram 3?
r. Joe has a few things he wants to say now.

Function	Formal	Informal
Greeting an audience		
Encouraging questions		
Introducing another speaker		
Addressing a specific audience member		
Introducing a topic		
Closing a presentation		
Drawing attention to an image		
Explaining a graph		
Presenting statistics		

20 Business Basics 2

2 SITUATIONAL DIALOGUE

1 Before reading the dialogue, use the information given below to answer the following questions.

Mr. Elliot — Ms. Sanders's supervisor
Ms. Sanders — A junior sales associate

MISSION
- To check Ms. Sanders's progress in preparing for an upcoming meeting
- To ask for your supervisor's advice about your presentation.

1. Look at the characters and describe the situation.
2. What is the relationship between the characters?
3. What do you think will happen next?

2 Practice the dialogue and answer the comprehension questions.

Overcoming a Fear of Public Speaking

Mr. Elliot: Good morning, Ms. Sanders. How is your presentation coming?

Ms. Sanders: I think I'm finished with the PowerPoint, but I'm a little nervous. If you could look it over, I'd be very grateful.

Mr. Elliot: Being nervous is only natural. Let me see what you've got done so far. We can begin by looking at the data you're going to use.

Ms. Sanders: Here you go, sir.

Mr. Elliot: Everything looks good, but I'm not sure if I understand this slide. It's a little cluttered.

Ms. Sanders: What you're asking is for me to simplify it?

Mr. Elliot: Yes. I think if you just changed the formatting a little bit it would be a lot easier to follow. How were you planning on closing the presentation?

Ms. Sanders: As a final point, I'd like to briefly review the key points of my presentation.

Mr. Elliot: That sounds perfect. I can't wait to see it in action. Don't be nervous you are well-prepared, and I think you're going to do great!

Ms. Sanders: Thank you for your help. I feel much better now.

Questions

1. Do you think it is impossible to overcome a fear of public speaking? Why or why not?
2. Describe an experience you have had with public speaking. Were you nervous? Explain.
3. What advice would you give Ms. Sanders to help her overcome her fear?

Lesson 3. Presentation Know-how

3 LANGUAGE FOCUS

••• KEY PATTERNS

Here are some key patterns that you can use when conducting or discussing presentations.

We can begin by looking at...
- the sales data from last quarter.
- some statistics about the project.
- the growth forecasts for next quarter.

As a final point, I'd like to...
- outline some of our goals.
- review the most recent sales figures.
- update you about our progress so far.

What you're asking is...
- where we got our information?
- what steps we will take?
- what progress our team has made?

4 SET THE STAGE

CASE SCENARIOS

Read each scenario and complete each stage.

1 Business Expressions

Read the expressions and write your own sentence using each expression.

at stake at risk; at issue or in question
Ex) Everything depends on this presentation. There is a lot at stake.
Sentence _____

see eye to eye to have similar views or attitudes about something
Ex) I think we have similar goals, so I'm sure we'll see eye to eye on this project.
Sentence _____

up-and-coming making good progress at something; likely to become successful
Ex) This is Fred Smith. He's an up-and-coming member of our design team.
_____

Scenario #1   Presenter   Investor

You are responsible for introducing your company to a potential investor. Briefly describe your company and its goals. The investor asks a question about your company's sales outlook for next year. Clarify the question and answer.

Stage 1. Brainstorm the mission of each character.
_____
_____

Stage 2. Role play.
Be sure to complete the mission of each character and use at least 2 key patterns.

Scenario #2   Employee 1 (Responsible for presenting team's research)
                 Employee 2 (Giving feedback)

You are responsible for presenting data about your sales team's progress over the past quarter. It is your first time performing this role, so you are a little nervous. Ask your more experienced co-worker for advice on what information to include and how to organize it.

Stage 1. Brainstorm the mission of each character.
_____
_____

Stage 2. Role play.
Be sure to complete the mission of each character and use at least 2 key patterns.

5 BUSINESS BASICS

Effective Presentation Skills

Presentations are key ways to build your career. While you are speaking, you are in the spotlight. For that block of time, you can either control or bore your audience. You can make the audience alert or apathetic. It is good to know what inputs make a presentation sizzling. Although technology can make the role of presenter easier, the two main resources are your own voice and body. Thus, the art of presentation can be divided into two main categories:
Voice (Verbal) + Body (Physical).

Speaking Error	Effect
Using "vocalized pauses" such as "er", "um", and "like"	• Leads the audience to believe the speaker's thoughts are not organized
Speaking too quickly	• Difficulty in understanding the contents • Doesn't allow time for the audience to reflect on the content
Creaky voice	• Unpleasant to listen to • Distracting
Trailing off at the end of sentences	• Deflates the energy and message • Sound boring and uninteresting; lacks "punch" and pizzazz
"Upward intonation" at the end of phrases / sentence (i.e. voice pitch goes higher)	• Makes statements sound like questions
Monotonous voice	• Extremely boring • Lacks cues for the audience to take note

Speaking Strength	Effect
Organization	• Each part has its own purpose which supports the main idea • Clear connection among ideas
Use of metaphor and analogy	• A concept that is hard to understand on its own becomes easy to understand
Pausing	• Lets the last word gain interest • Audience has time to take in information
Gestures and movement	• Limited and controlled movement can grab the audience's attention and emphasizes key aspects of the speech
Visual aids	• Humans can remember pictures much more easily than abundant words

Share Your Thoughts

1. Which of the negative habits above do you think would most ruin a speech? What advice would you give to someone who commits such an error?

2. Have you ever watched a famous speech on YouTube or as part of class? What made the speech remarkable? Please list all the qualities.

3. Which do you think would be harder: giving a speech to your fellow employees; or giving a speech to a group of people unknown to you?

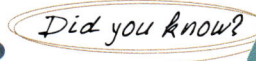

Did you know?

❶ In a presentation, facts are 20 times more likely to be remembered if they are part of a story.

❷ A memorable, vivid image added to a presentation will make the audience remember 95% of that what they hear and see at that moment.

Lesson 3. Presentation Know-how

6 NUMBERS & FACTS

Cultural Note

Filipinos often greet each other with the 'eyebrow flash', which is a quick lifting of the eyebrows.

Look at the image above to answer the following questions.

1. Are you somebody who suffers from anxiety over public speaking? Please describe your level of comfort / discomfort with public speaking.

2. Confidence in public speaking is a valuable skill that companies generally encourage their employees to acquire and develop.
What kind of program would be good for gaining presentation confidence?

3. What percentage of people do not have a fear of public speaking? Do you think that public speaking ability is a natural gift, or is it a taught skill?

7 REVIEW & PREVIEW

Share 3 new things you learned from this lesson:

1.

2.

3.

 Sneak Peek

1. Do you consider yourself to have a structured work mode, or do you consider yourself to be adaptable to change according to the situation and need?

2. Do you think that it is possible to be "too thankful" at work?

LESSON 04

UNIT 1. PROFESSIONAL COMMUNICATOR

Situational Communication Strategies

Overview

- [ ] Getting Started
- [ ] Situational Dialogue
- [ ] Language Focus
- [ ] Set the Stage
- [ ] Business Basics
- [ ] Numbers and Facts

[Learning Objectives] Upon completion of this lesson, you will be able to…
- apply different communicational strategies in various situations; such as showing sympathy, confronting problems, and giving compliments

1 GETTING STARTED

1 Warm up

Let's open the floor. What are your opinions?

01.
What are some situations where you might need to show sympathy? How would you react?

02.
Have you ever had a conflict with a co-worker? Describe how you confronted the problem.

03.
Why do you think it is important to be prepared to communicate in different situations? How can you build your confidence doing so?

2 Formal vs. Informal

Write the correct phrases in the formal or informal column of the table according to the tone.

a. I'm so sorry to hear about your problem.
b. Could you use some assistance?
c. Could I speak with you for a minute?
d. You seem to be upset about something.
e. I was concerned that something was wrong.
f. What seems to be the problem?
g. I was very upset to hear about your situation.
h. I believe I have an answer to your problem.
i. Your job performance has been excellent lately.
j. Need some help?
k. Little help, please?
l. Nice work!
m. Got some time?
n. What's wrong?
o. I've got an idea!
p. I'm worried about you.
q. You look tired today.
r. Would you mind assisting me?

Function	Formal	Informal
Expressing sympathy		
Commenting on mood		
Asking about a problem		
Complimenting one's work		
Expressing concern		
Offering help		
Asking for help		
Asking someone to talk		
Offering a solution		

Lesson 4. Situational Communication Strategies

2 SITUATIONAL DIALOGUE

1 Before reading the dialogue, use the information given below to answer the following questions.

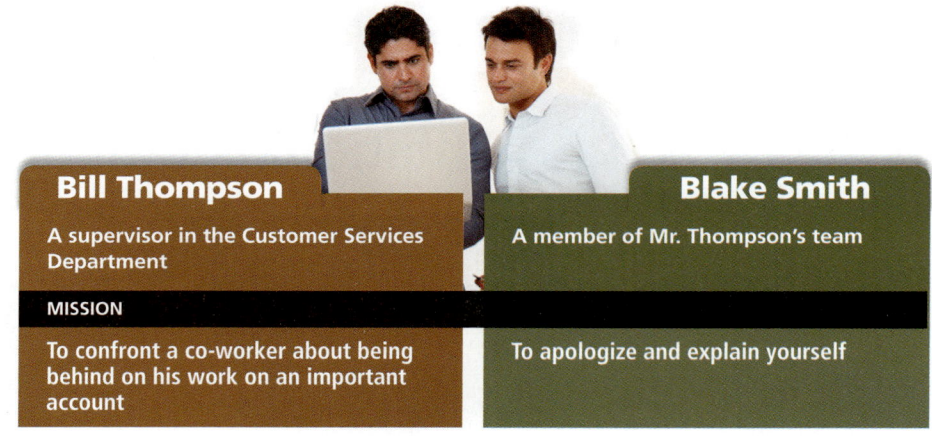

Bill Thompson
A supervisor in the Customer Services Department

Blake Smith
A member of Mr. Thompson's team

MISSION

To confront a co-worker about being behind on his work on an important account

To apologize and explain yourself

1. Look at the characters and describe the situation.
2. What is the relationship between the characters?
3. What do you think will happen next?

2 Practice the dialogue and answer the comprehension questions.

Confronting a Problem

Bill Thompson: Hey, Blake. How are things going?

Blake Smith: Not so good. It's been a stressful week.

Bill Thompson: I'm sorry to hear about your situation. I know it must be difficult to come into work feeling sick.

Blake Smith: I'm feeling much better today actually just a little stressed.

Bill Thompson: You look a little overwhelmed today. How are you doing on the Jefferson account?

Blake Smith: I've had some problems, but I'm optimistic that I can catch up soon.

Bill Thompson: I want to talk to you about that. While you were out sick, I had to take a look at your records, and I was surprised to see how far behind you have fallen. I think that it might be better if we let someone else work on that account.

Blake Smith: I'm very sorry to hear that. I thought I could fix things by myself.

Bill Thompson: I know and I just want to let you know that everyone thinks that you are doing a great job. Remember that you can always ask for help if you have a problem.

Blake Smith: I understand. I'm sorry that I didn't ask for help sooner.

Questions

1. Is it easy to ask for help in your workplace? Why or why not?
2. Do you think Mr. Thompson handled the situation well? Explain.
3. Describe a time that you needed help at work. Who did you ask? How did it make you feel?

3 LANGUAGE FOCUS

••• KEY PATTERNS

Here are some key patterns that you can use to communicate in various situations.

I'm sorry to hear about...
- your problem.
- the delay.
- your mother's passing.

You look... today
- much better
- a little tired
- great

I want to talk to you about...
- your great work on the project.
- the upcoming presentation.
- the issues your team has been having.

1 Business Expressions

Read the expressions and write your own sentence using each expression.

a rule of thumb a guide or principle, based on experience
Ex) As a rule of thumb, I avoid talking about controversial topics with business partners.
Sentence

to be swamped to be burdened with work
Ex) I'm sorry that I couldn't call back sooner. I was swamped earlier.
Sentence

slack off to waste time or avoid work
Ex) Don't slack off now. We need to finish this report.
Sentence

4 SET THE STAGE

CASE SCENARIOS

Read each scenario and complete each stage.

Scenario #1
 Team Leader
Team Member whose mother recently passed away

You are a team leader in the Marketing Department. One of your subordinates recently took some time off because of a death in his or her family. Welcome your co-worker back to the office by showing your sympathy and offering help. Listen to your co-worker describe his or her situation.

Stage 1. Brainstorm the mission of each character.

Stage 2. Role play.
Be sure to complete the mission of each character and use at least 2 key patterns.

Scenario #2
 Employee 1
 Co-worker who has recently received a promotion

One of your team members has just received a promotion to a managerial position at another branch. Compliment your co-worker and let him or her know what a pleasure it has been working together. Discuss your co-worker's future plans.

Stage 1. Brainstorm the mission of each character.

Stage 2. Role play.
Be sure to complete the mission of each character and use at least 2 key patterns.

5 BUSINESS BASICS

FUN FACTS

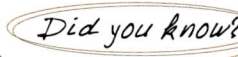

❶ Approximately 48% of white evangelical Christians report experiencing or witnessing religious bias in the workplace.

❷ Employees view inadequate staffing as the #1 source of stress in their jobs, which could lead to conflict among co-workers.

Situational Communication Strategies

In life, **communication** is how we adapt, respond to, and engage with ever-changing situations, relationships, needs, and stresses. How we communicate is just as important as the decisions we make. Having a ready supply of responses can make you a successful communicator for a variety of situations. The most crucial situations which demand the most apt and suave response are situations of conflict.

Organizational development researchers, Kenneth W. Thomas and Ralph H. Kilmann, created an "instrument" that allows people to measure in what manner they are likely to resolve conflict. However, they do stress that no single person has just one style. People use various modes to handle conflict according to their dispositions and situations. Where do you fit below?

Thomas-Kilmann Conflict Mode Instrument	
Trait	**Description**
Competing	Power-oriented mode in which you use whatever tactics and power you have to assert your position and win.
	Not dealing with an issue, such as postponing, making excuses, delegating to other departments, etc.
	A middle ground that satisfies needs for the present. However, the solution might not be dynamic or long term.
	Yielding to another. Might be a form of sacrifice if you would really prefer an opposite choice. Can cause regret.
	Finding a deep and creative solution that represents synergy and satisfies both sides in an appealing way.

Share Your Thoughts

1. Write the correct trait for each description.

   Collaborating / Accommodating / Compromising / Avoiding

2. Which trait are you most likely to use in conflict situations? Why are you most likely to act that way?

3. Do you think companies should provide a 'procedure' for handling conflict? Why or why not?

6 NUMBERS & FACTS

In Thailand, never place your arm over the back of a chair in which someone is sitting. Such an act is considered offensive. Also, do not pat someone's shoulders or back.

Look at the image above to answer the following questions.

1. Have you ever had a project fail due to conflict? If that ever happened, how would you deal with the consequences of the failed project?

2. Have you or anybody you have known ever missed work due to conflict? Do you think that conflict is a legitimate reason to miss work or "take a sick day"?

3. Have you ever decided just to "let go" of a conflict? What are your criteria for deciding that a conflict is just "not worth it"?

7 REVIEW & PREVIEW

Share 3 new things you learned from this lesson:

1. ....

2. ....

3. ....

 ▶ **Sneak Peek**

1. Does negotiating during a business proposal make you nervous? What steps do you take to get ready for negotiating?

2. Have you ever had to "push back" and resist someone else's proposal? How would you try to turn a proposal in your favor?

CASE STUDY 1
Powerful Communication Elevator Speeches

Background

Communicating well in business means being able to explain things quickly and clearly. A good way to engage your audience is to start with an "elevator speech"–a short, engaging summary of your key points. The name comes from the idea that if a short conversation in an elevator is interesting enough, the listener will find a way to continue it after the doors open. This strategy can work well for introductions, presentations and making small talk.

> You know how most business people use PowerPoint but few of them use it well? Well, bad PowerPoint can cause all kinds of problems—deals that don't close, good ideas that get ignored, time that gets wasted making unattractive PowerPoints. My company teaches businesses to use PowerPoint to their advantage—to close deals, draw attention to great ideas and to use time on more important projects.

Tips

1. Keep it short. (60 seconds at most)
2. Make it easy to understand by using everyday language. (Don't assume the listener understands industry jargon.)
3. Utilize a question to gauge attention.
   Ex) Have you ever purchased a computer online?

UNIT 1.
Professional Communicator

Tasks

01 Imagine you are a representative from a coffee chain attending a conference for prospective franchise investors. You will meet a lot of people and need to be able to explain your company quickly and in an interesting way. Develop an elevator speech to break the ice with the people that you meet and demonstrate why they should invest in your franchise.

About your company

What are your company's strengths

What can your company do for them

How will you accomplish it

02 Now, share your "elevator speech" with a partner. Exchange feedback about what went well and what needs more work.

03 Think about your company, department, or team. Prepare an elevator speech to introduce your area of expertise to potential investors or clients.

UNIT 1. Professional Communicator **31**

UNIT 2. WINNING NEGOTIATOR

LESSON 05
Proposal & Negotiation

Overview
- [ ] Getting Started
- [ ] Situational Dialogue
- [ ] Language Focus
- [ ] Set the Stage
- [ ] Business Basics
- [ ] Numbers and Facts

[Learning Objectives] Upon completion of this lesson, you will be able to...
- enhance knowledge and skills related to business negotiation and articulate your position
- make business proposals and counter-proposals

1 GETTING STARTED

1 Warm up

Let's open the floor.
What are your opinions?

01.
Describe an experience when you had to negotiate for something. How did you approach the task?

02.
Do you consider yourself a good negotiator? Why or why not?

03.
What skills do you think are most important for business negotiations? Explain.

2 Formal vs. Informal

Write the correct phrases in the formal or informal column of the table according to the tone.

a. That sounds great!
b. I've got something for you.
c. I can accept your terms.
d. You'll be interested in this.
e. No, thanks.
f. What else?
g. Let me think it over.
h. I'm sorry, but I can't agree to that.
i. Have you considered trying our newer model?
j. You should try this stock.
k. I understand your concern, but you don't need to worry.
l. Could I please have a day or two to think about it?
m. What do you think about extending your contract?
n. I would recommend diversifying your portfolio.
o. I have an opportunity to discuss with you.
p. Could you please give me some more information about the product?
q. Don't worry. It's not too good to be true.
r. You might be interested in this investment.

Function	Formal	Informal
Introducing an idea		
Inviting interest		
Recommending something		
Addressing doubt		
Hinting at a request		
Asking for more time		
Asking for more information		
Refusing		
Agreeing		

2 SITUATIONAL DIALOGUE

1 Before reading the dialogue, use the information given below to answer the following questions.

Mr. Sterling — Human Resources Team Member
MISSION: To negotiate the terms of Ms. Gavins's contract.

Ms. Gavins — Job Applicant
To let Mr. Sterling know about your specific needs before committing to your new job.

1. Look at the characters and describe the situation.
2. What is the relationship between the characters?
3. What do you think will happen next?

2 Practice the dialogue and answer the comprehension questions.

Contract Negotiation

Mr. Sterling: Thank you for meeting me here today, Ms. Gavins. I'm excited to hear that you might be interested in joining our team.

Ms. Gavins: Yes, I've heard a lot of good things about your company, and I feel that I would be a good fit here.

Mr. Sterling: That's good to hear. I've asked you here to negotiate the terms of your contract. I know you had settled on a salary with Mr. Bale in your interview, but I need to address some of your other requests. I heard you had some special vacation needs.

Ms. Gavins: Yes. I know that new employees only get one week of vacation a year, but I will need a little more this year. My sister is getting married in Canada this May. Also, I promised to spend the holidays with my husband's family in Europe, so I'll need some time off at Christmas as well.

Mr. Sterling: Those are good reasons to take time off. How much vacation will you need?

Ms. Gavins: I'm thinking of two and a half weeks: a week for the wedding and a week and a half for Christmas.

Mr. Sterling: That is a lot more than normal, but it might be possible. What do you think about taking the Christmas holiday unpaid?

Ms. Gavins: I suppose that would be okay. I understand it's a lot to ask as a new employee.

Mr. Sterling: That's good to hear. If you don't have any more questions, then I'll draft a contract for you to sign right away.

Ms. Gavins: I think you've addressed all of my concerns. I look forward to seeing the contract.

Questions

1. Do you think Ms. Gavins's vacation demands are reasonable? Why or why not?
2. What are the most important considerations when negotiating for a new job? Explain.
3. Do you have any experience negotiating contract terms? Did you accomplish what you had set in mind? Explain.

Lesson 5. Proposal & Negotiation

3 LANGUAGE FOCUS

••• KEY PATTERNS

Here are some key patterns that you can use when discussing business proposals.

You might be interested in...
- our new product.
- this idea.
- joining us for this project.

I'm thinking of...
- our long-term goals.
- the best option for us.
- trying to get a little more money.

What do you think about...
- giving us a discount?
- extending the contract period?
- lowering the interest rate?

1 Business Expressions

Read the expressions and write your own sentence using each expression.

to get ahead of one self to plan or do something which is not yet appropriate
Ex) Don't get ahead of yourself. You still need to interview for the job, so you shouldn't be planning to move yet.
Sentence

double-check go over something twice to ensure it is accurate
Ex) Let me double-check those figures before we send the report.
Sentence

on a roll experiencing a prolonged spell of success or good luck
Ex) I can't believe you got them to sign the contract. You're really on a roll lately.
Sentence

4 SET THE STAGE

CASE SCENARIOS

Read each scenario and complete each stage.

Scenario #1

Role A: **Team Leader in the Sales Department**
Role B: **Sales Department Head**

You are a team leader in the Sales Department. In your two years in the position, your team has tripled sales volume and greatly expanded its customer base within its sales region. Request a raise from your department head and provide evidence to support your request for more money.

Stage 1. Brainstorm the mission of each character.

Stage 2. Role play.
Be sure to complete the mission of each character and use at least 2 key patterns.

Scenario #2

Role A: **Account Manager from Ace Investments**
Role B: **Client who is interested in expanding his or her portfolio**

You are an employee at an investment firm and you have been tasked with promoting a new investment opportunity to one of your clients. The investment is for an up-and-coming tech firm that is developing software for financial forecasting. The software is expected to revolutionize the finance industry. Propose the idea and explain why it is a good choice.

Stage 1. Brainstorm the mission of each character.

Stage 2. Role play.
Be sure to complete the mission of each character and use at least 2 key patterns.

5 BUSINESS BASICS

Proposal and Negotiation

Negotiation is a crucial aspect of business. Having a skilled negotiator on your team can protect your assets and further your interests. A weak negotiator can lose ground and cause entanglements. In contrast, a skilled negotiator can drive deals and bargains that position the company for success and contain favorable economic terms.

Adept negotiation requires fluency in a few skills. Having a developed negotiation toolkit can allow your side to maintain its interests while also adding value to your new partner. Which skill would you rate most highly for negotiations?

Negotiation Skills

Skill	Rank	Reason
Bold Opening: start with an aggressive bid		
Preparation and Research: understand the other side		
Patience: avoid rushing		
Positive Attitude: focus on goals instead of risks		
Eagerness: Don't want to lose the deal		
Empathy: Sympathize with the other side		
Willingness to Yield: Ability to give in on low priority issues		

Share Your Thoughts

1. Fill in the table above with a rank and reason for each skill. Which quality is your #1? Why?

2. When you enter a negotiation are you more focused on what you might gain or on what you might lose? Explain.

3. Some negotiation strategists believe that the less you say, the better. How much information should you share during a negotiation?

FUN FACTS

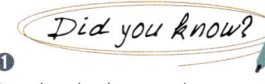

❶ People who have an income greater than $75,000 USD a year are not significantly happier in their day-to-day lives.

❷ When economist Linda C. Babcock asked women and men to choose a metaphor to describe negotiations: women chose "going to the dentist" while men chose "winning a ballgame".

Lesson 5. Proposal & Negotiation

When speaking to someone in ***Hong Kong***, try to limit blinking. Noticeable blinking during a conversation is taken as a sign of boredom and disrespect.

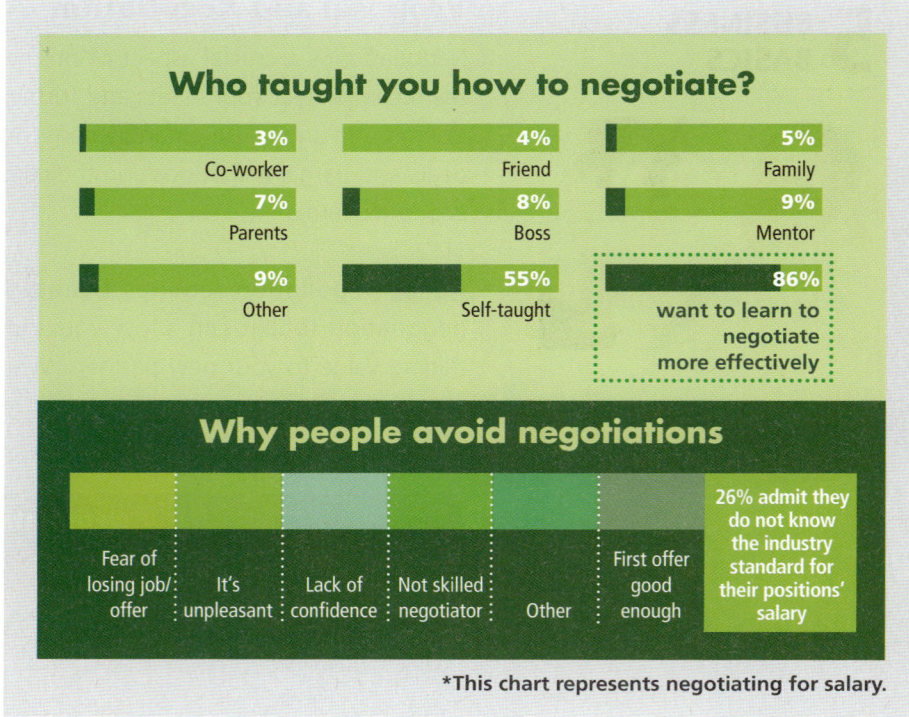

Look at the image above to answer the following questions.

1. What percentage of individuals are self-taught at negotiating their salary? Are you part of this number?

2. Give a short presentation on why people might avoid negotiating. What reasons do you think make up the "Other" category?

3. What conclusions can you make regarding the fact that 86% of people would like to negotiate more effectively? *(For example, do you think this number indicates that many people think that they are underpaid?)*

Share 3 new things you learned from this lesson:

1.

2.

3.

7 REVIEW & PREVIEW

 **Sneak Peek**

1. Before making major business decisions, how do you determine what the consequences for each decision might be?

2. How do you rate yourself at being able to predict the outcome of decisions? Please explain your self-rating with examples.

36 Business Basics 2

LESSON 06

Tackling Problems

UNIT 2. WINNING NEGOTIATOR

Overview

- [ ] Getting Started
- [ ] Situational Dialogue
- [ ] Language Focus
- [ ] Set the Stage
- [ ] Business Basics
- [ ] Numbers and Facts

[Learning Objectives] Upon completion of this lesson, you will be able to…
- discuss solutions to business problems and consider the consequences of possible course of action
- find compromises in conflict solutions

1 GETTING STARTED

1 Warm up

Let's open the floor.
What are your opinions?

01.
What are some cultural differences that you have observed when interacting with foreigners? Explain.

02.
Why do you think it is important to be aware of cultural differences when interacting with people from other cultures? Support your opinion with details.

03.
How would you explain your country's communication style to a foreign visitor? Are there any types of body language or gestures that they should be aware of?

2 Formal vs. Informal

Write the correct phrases in the formal or informal column of the table according to the tone.

a. In the future, you should be more careful.
b. We should research more and reevaluate the situation.
c. There's something wrong with the data.
d. I could offer you a discount if you purchase more units.
e. It might be helpful to change our approach.
f. We are both entitled to an opinion.
g. If the negotiation fails, we will lose a great deal of money.
h. I just became aware of an error in our report.
i. You can think that if you want.
j. If things don't work out, we will go out of business.
k. Let's try that.
l. I can meet you halfway on this.
m. It seems to be working.
n. We should try calling him directly.
o. This deal will benefit both of us.
p. Looks good so far.
q. Next time, double-check your facts.
r. We can both say yes to this.

Function	Formal	Informal
Bringing up a mistake		
Suggesting a compromise		
Offering gentle criticism		
Considering risks		
Agreeing to disagree		
Finding common ground		
Offering a solution		
Settling on a course of action		
Evaluating a solution		

Lesson 6. Tackling Problems

2 SITUATIONAL DIALOGUE

1 Before reading the dialogue, use the information given below to answer the following questions.

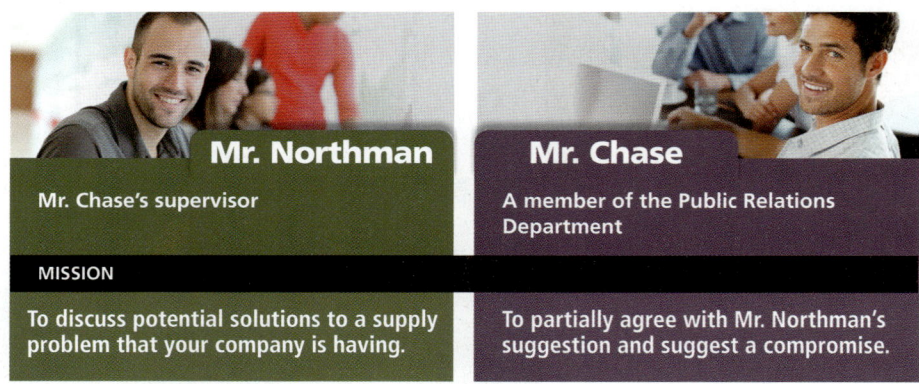

Mr. Northman — Mr. Chase's supervisor
MISSION: To discuss potential solutions to a supply problem that your company is having.

Mr. Chase — A member of the Public Relations Department
To partially agree with Mr. Northman's suggestion and suggest a compromise.

1. Look at the characters and describe the situation.
2. What is the relationship between the characters?
3. What do you think will happen next?

2 Practice the dialogue and answer the comprehension questions.

Suggesting Compromises

Mr. Northman: How's the announcement coming? Did you figure out how to tell the customers about the supply problem?

Mr. Chase: I'm not sure. With the recall, it seems like we can't avoid a delay. I suppose we could just let the customers know that the shipments are going to be late.

Mr. Northman: It looks like it's going to be solved soon. Announcing a delay like this might cause problems. If we're seen as being unstable, this could lead to losing clients to our competitor.

Mr. Chase: You're right, but what other choice do we have? I think we should just tell them as soon as possible. It would save time to tell them now.

Mr. Northman: Telling them early is a good idea, but we need to have something to offer them for the inconvenience.

Mr. Chase: What were you thinking?

Mr. Northman: How about a discount on their next order? Just to show our appreciation for their understanding. That way they will be more likely to order again.

Mr. Chase: That's a great idea. We need to check with Mr. Jones.

Mr. Northman: Sounds good. Why don't you write a rough draft to show him?

Mr. Chase: I'll start on that now. Thanks for your help.

Questions

1. What do you think of the men's approach? What would you do differently?
2. Do you often have to work on team projects? When is compromise necessary?
3. Do you find it easy to compromise? Why or why not?

3 LANGUAGE FOCUS

••• KEY PATTERNS

Here are some key patterns that you can use when discussing solutions to business problems.

I suppose we can...
- try a different approach.
- ask Bill for some advice.
- review the data one more time.

It would save time to...
- work together.
- use the new program.
- combine these two tasks.

This could lead to...
- a serious delay if we can't fix the problem.
- big success for our team.
- issues later.

4 SET THE STAGE

CASE SCENARIOS

Read each scenario and complete each stage.

1 Business Expressions

Read the expressions and write your own sentence using each expression.

keep track of to be fully aware of or informed about something
Ex) I've been keeping track of your project and I'm really impressed with the progress that you've made so far.
Sentence

over one's head beyond someone's ability to understand
Ex) Could you please help me with this? I'm really in over my head.
Sentence

step into someone's shoes to take over a job or some role from someone
Ex) I'm going to have to step into Frank's shoes while he's on his business trip.
Sentence

Scenario #1

👤 Department Head of the Customer Services Department
👤 Team Leader with another job offer

You are the department head of the Customer Service Department. One of your most valued team leaders has come to you because they are considering leaving their position for a job offer at another firm. Assure them what a valuable employee they are and ask for details in order to match the other firm's job offer.

Stage 1. Brainstorm the mission of each character.

Stage 2. Role play.
Be sure to complete the mission of each character and use at least 2 key patterns.

Scenario #2

 Team Member 1 (in favor of the investment)
 Team Member 2 (worried about the risk)

You are a member of the Research and Development Department. You and a co-worker are evaluating a new electronic car that you are considering investing in. The investment would require a great deal of capital, but if it is successful, it could yield a lot of profit. You are in favor of the investment, but your co-worker thinks it is too risky. Discuss the pros and cons of the investment.

Stage 1. Brainstorm the mission of each character.

Stage 2. Role play.
Be sure to complete the mission of each character and use at least 2 key patterns.

Lesson 6. Tackling Problems

BUSINESS BASICS 5

FUN FACTS

Did you know?

❶ Only 2% of sales occur when two parties meet for the first time.

❷ Approximately 44% of sales people give up after the first "no".

Tackling Problems

A business is a living institution. A business must face challenges, and changes, as well as adapt, move forward, and make decisions all the time. However, every "decisions crossroads" is fraught with the unknown. What you decide upon and how you act in response to problems will determine the very life and success of your company.

One of the challenges in making decisions is that there are certain 'traps' that can impair thinking. Look at the table below. Which trap do you consider most dangerous?

Hidden Traps in Decision-Making		
Mistake	**Explanation**	**Biggest Danger for You** (Ranking #)
Overly Cautious	Guards too much against unlikely and improbable outcomes	#
Over Confident	Underestimates likely dangers; overestimate ability	#
Impressionable	Overly influenced by current events	#
Confirmation Bias	Acts in a way to support "what you already believe"	#
Saving Face	Invests in things that are outwardly impressionable; doesn't deal with the underlying situation	#
Anchoring	The first news/data/proposition dominates all thoughts	#
Status Quo	Prefers keeping things unchanged	#

Share Your Thoughts

1. Fill in the table. Rank each mistake from the most negative impact to the least negative impact. Which behavior do you see as most destructive to the decision-making process? Explain.

2. Which do you think is more dangerous: taking too little time or too much time to make a decision?

6 NUMBERS & FACTS

Cultural Note

Some cultures, like Korean and Spanish, enjoy sharing food during a meal. In **Bangladesh**, however, you should never transfer food from your own plate to another person's, even a family member or close acquaintance.

Reality Gap

There is a reality gap between how good managers think they are and how effective they actually are.

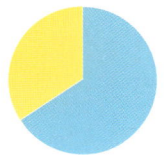 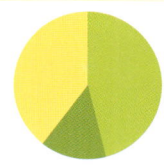 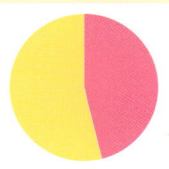 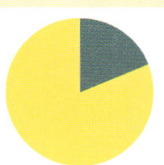

72% of employees report a lack of leadership and management skills in their organizations.

80% of managers think their staff are satisfied with them Only **58%** of employees agree.

24% of employees say they meet with managers at least twice a month to talk about workload and objectives.

58% employees satisfied with their managers.

Look at the image above to answer the following questions.

1. What percentage of people "report a lack of leadership and management in their organizations"?

2. Please use the chart to explain the difference that exists between how managers view themselves and how the employees view the managers.

3. Can you make any connection between the satisfaction rate and the percentage of people who meet with their managers per month to discuss "workload and objectives"?

7 REVIEW & PREVIEW

Share 3 new things you learned from this lesson:

1.

2.

3.

 Sneak Peek

1. If you were to have a business negotiation with a foreign company, what do you think would be challenging about the process?

2. Do you think that there are cultural attributes to negotiating? If so, what might they be?

LESSON 07

UNIT 2. WINNING NEGOTIATOR

International Negotiations

Overview

- [ ] Getting Started
- [ ] Situational Dialogue
- [ ] Language Focus
- [ ] Set the Stage
- [ ] Business Basics
- [ ] Numbers and Facts

[Learning Objectives] Upon completion of this lesson, you will be able to…
- handle cultural differences during the negotiating process
- recognize different negotiation styles

1 GETTING STARTED

1 Warm up

Let's open the floor.
What are your opinions?

01.
Describe the negotiating process in your country. Are there any things that you feel are unique to your local business culture?

02.
What kind of advice would you give a foreigner negotiating in your country? Why?

03.
What do you think is the most important factor to understand before entering into a business relationship with a foreign company?

2 Formal vs. Informal

Write the correct phrases in the formal or informal column of the table according to the tone.

a. You're right about that.
b. You raised a good point.
c. We aren't interested.
d. Is this right?
e. We'll need to check with the board.
f. What's your opinion on the matter?
g. We can settle for a 5% discount.
h. I can't accept the terms of your offer.
i. We don't do that in our country.
j. Let's think this over until Monday.
k. I'd like to hear some more about that.
l. I'll need to get approval from the head office.
m. There seems to be a cultural difference.
n. Could you please confirm some of those details?
o. I think it's best we take another day to consider our options.
p. Would you consider accepting a little less?
q. What do you think about settling for $20 a meter?
r. We can accept your offer if you meet this demand.

Function	Formal	Informal
Noting a difference		
Offering a condition		
Asking to seek approval		
Making a counteroffer		
Asking to confirm		
Disagreeing		
Offering to listen		
Agreeing to compromise		
Extending a negotiation		

2 SITUATIONAL DIALOGUE

1 Before reading the dialogue, use the information given below to answer the following questions.

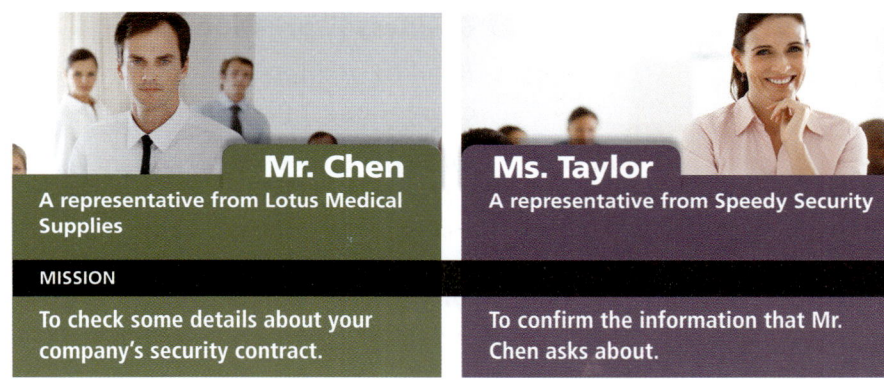

Mr. Chen — A representative from Lotus Medical Supplies

MISSION: To check some details about your company's security contract.

Ms. Taylor — A representative from Speedy Security

MISSION: To confirm the information that Mr. Chen asks about.

1. Look at the characters and describe the situation.
2. What is the relationship between the characters?
3. What do you think will happen next?

2 Practice the dialogue and answer the comprehension questions.

Checking and Confirming

Mr. Chen: I think we're almost finished here.
I just need to finalize a few details before we agree to the contract.
As you know, we had some conflict last time,
so our team has reevaluated some of our needs.

Ms. Taylor: Yes, of course. I'd be interested to hear about what you have decided.

Mr. Chen: First of all, can we agree on the length of the contract period? We decided to accept your company's offer of two years.

Ms. Taylor: Thank you for your understanding. I understand that your company initially wanted something shorter, but that's the best I can offer at this time. Our company has a strict two-year minimum policy for new customers.

Mr. Chen: Also, can we confirm that service will start on October 1st?

Ms. Taylor: Yes, that won't be a problem.

Mr. Chen: I think that was all I needed to check. When can you have the contract ready?

Ms. Taylor: I will fax over a copy later this afternoon.

Mr. Chen: Perfect. Thank you for meeting with me today.

Ms. Taylor: It was my pleasure. I look forward to working with you.

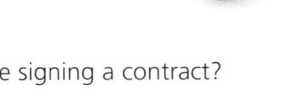

Questions

1. What information did Mr. Chen need to confirm?
2. Why do you think it is important to confirm details before signing a contract?
3. What are some other details that might need to be confirmed? How could you ask about them?

3 LANGUAGE FOCUS

••• KEY PATTERNS

Here are some key patterns that you can use when discussing cultural differences related to the negotiation process.

I understand that...
- you want to make a counteroffer.
- you don't want to compromise.
- you are interested in importing some of our products.

I'd be interested to hear about...
- any ideas that you have.
- alternative courses of actions.
- your demands.

Can we agree on...
- a way to approach the situation?
- a form of payment?
- the terms of the agreement?

1 Business Expressions

Read the expressions and write your own sentence using each expression.

jot down write briefly or hurriedly
Ex) Let me just jot down your phone number.
Sentence

nitty-gritty the practical details of a subject or situation
Ex) Let's get down to the nitty-gritty. We need to get this project done.
Sentence

explore all avenues to try everything in order to find a solution
Ex) We need to explore all avenues before giving up. I'm sure we can find a solution.
Sentence

4 SET THE STAGE

CASE SCENARIOS

Read each scenario and complete each stage.

Scenario #1

 Role A: **Representative from Blue Sky Televisions**
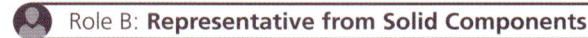 Role B: **Representative from Solid Components**

Your country has just entered into a partnership with a Chinese electronics company. They will be supplying some components for your company's new television line. You are hoping to receive a discount based on the volume of purchases. Make small talk and then discuss the basic terms of the agreement.

Stage 1. Brainstorm the mission of each character.

Stage 2. Role play.
Be sure to complete the mission of each character and use at least 2 key patterns.

Scenario #2

 Role A: **Team Member 1**
 Role B: **Team Member 2**

Your company is beginning negotiations with a potential supplier in Estonia. No one on the team has experience negotiating with Estonians, so you and a partner are responsible for finding out as much as possible about the country's business culture. Before you begin your research, decide what is important to know. Determine what kind of cultural information you need in order to successively negotiate with the company.

Stage 1. Brainstorm the mission of each character.

Stage 2. Role play.
Be sure to complete the mission of each character and use at least 2 key patterns.

5 BUSINESS BASICS

International Negotiations

One of the first rules in international negotiations is never to assume that the processes and rules abroad are just like your own. Particularly, laws regarding corporate joint ventures can vary greatly by country. Some of the main concerns to bear in mind are: Who are the main decision-makers? What are their roles and responsibilities? How are decisions made? Who else, such as ministries, officials, or competitors, could interfere with or influence the decision?

Because cultures vary in their decision-making procedures, customs, outlook, and rule of law, it is good to take a look at these aspects before entering a negotiation.

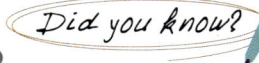

Need to Know

Skill	Reason
Cooperative Process vs. Competitive Process	Win-win outlook vs. Win-lose outlook
Contract Substance: General Principles vs. Specific Details	Basic outline of relationship vs. Exact directions for behavior
Contract Enforcement	Strict adherence vs. General agreement open to change and renegotiation
Hierarchy vs. Consensus	A few key power players can decide vs. Many groups and interests must decide together
Negotiation: Ritual vs. Active Engagement	The contract table: Sign what has been agreed upon behind the scenes vs. Open new dialogue and discussion
(Your Key Point)	(Your Explanation)

FUN FACTS

Did you know?

❶ Approximately 50% of the ownership of Domino's Pizza was once traded for a used Volkswagen Beetle (small car).

❷ Almost 75% of successful sales are directly as the result of an enticing and persuasive opening statement.

Share Your Thoughts

1. What information do you think is important to know before entering a cross-cultural negotiation? Why?
   Fill in the last row for the table above and share your answers.

2. For some companies and cultures, doing business is about establishing trust and relationships first. How do you feel about this process of making relationships first?

3. In Western cultures, companies might contact each other directly in order to start a business negotiation. In contrast, for some Eastern cultures, first introductions occur through intermediaries. Please explain the pros and cons of each side.

6 NUMBERS & FACTS

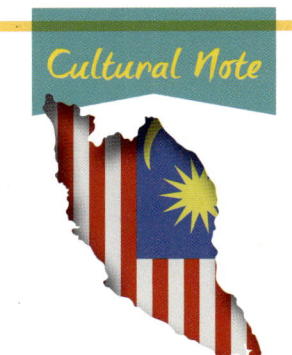

Cultural Note

Malaysia is composed of three ethnic groups: Malay, Chinese, and Indian. The practitioners of Islam typically have a prayer rug in their home or office. Be aware of such a special rug and avoid touching it. Also, Indian Malaysians shake their head side to side to show agreement, which to a Western looks like the "no" sign.

Use the above chart to answer the following questions.

Country	Rapport	Positioning	Persuasion	Compromise	Agreement
USA	15.7	15.1	29.9	21.7	16.0
China	24.9	25.1	15.0	5.1	25.5
Latin America	33.3	11.6	26.6	11.6	16.0
France& Italy	15.1	12.5 1	15.0	15.0	46.0
Germany	10.2	5.1	30.1	27.5	17.5
Japan	26.6	20.1	10.1	11.6	25.0

Stages of negotiation by culture
* Estimated average percentage of time divided into each activity

Look at the chart above to answer the following questions.

1. What percentage of French and Italian meetings does the "Agreement" stage comprise?

2. Which countries' business cultures seem to value "Rapport" more highly in the negotiating process? Use the data to support your answer.

3. Chinese negotiations typically spend 5.1% of the time on the "Compromise" stage compared to 27.5% in German ones. What do you think this says about the two countries' business cultures?

7 REVIEW & PREVIEW

Share 3 new things you learned from this lesson:

1.

2.

3.

 ▶ **Let's Think**

1. What skills do you think are most valuable in being able to persuade the other side during a negotiation?

2. One negotiation trick is for one side to walk away at the final moment in order to stun the other side, and make them panic.
If this tactic was used against you, how you would you react?

LESSON 08

UNIT 2. WINNING NEGOTIATOR

Taking a Position

Overview

- [ ] Getting Started
- [ ] Situational Dialogue
- [ ] Language Focus
- [ ] Set the Stage
- [ ] Business Basics
- [ ] Numbers and Facts

[Learning Objectives] Upon completion of this lesson, you will be able to…
- state/clarify your position and persuade others to support your side
- close a negotiation

1 GETTING STARTED

1 Warm up

Let's open the floor. What are your opinions?

01.
Have you ever had to take a stance in a meeting? How did you persuade others to support your side?

02.
What strategies do you think are key in convincing others? Explain.

03.
Why is it important to be able to state your position clearly? How can you achieve this?

2 Formal vs. Informal

Write the correct phrases in the formal or informal column of the table according to the tone.

a. You're right, but I think we need to do more.
b. Let's think this over.
c. I think you've got to change the logo.
d. I think that's all.
e. Any thoughts?
f. With that, let's close our negotiation.
g. You can trust me on this.
h. Please meet me halfway on this.
i. I think this matter needs further discussion.
j. It is my opinion that raising the price is the best course of action.
k. Research proves a clear correlation between the two factors.
l. I'm interested in hearing your thoughts on the matter.
m. I believe strongly that this is the correct decision.
n. I meant we need more time.
o. What I intended to say is that we need to find more funding.
p. This study says we need a more direct sales method.
q. Could you please try to consider what we are asking?
r. Your view is correct, but try to understand my point of view.

Function	Formal	Informal
Stating a position		
Clarifying a statement		
Providing evidence		
Showing understanding		
Asking for feedback		
Requesting more consideration		
Maintaining opinions		
Asking for agreement		
Closing a negotiation		

Lesson 8. Taking a Position

2 SITUATIONAL DIALOGUE

1 Before reading the dialogue, use the information given below to answer the following questions.

1. Look at the characters and describe the situation.
2. What is the relationship between the characters?
3. What do you think will happen next?

2 Practice the dialogue and answer the comprehension questions.

Making a Stance

Mr. Roberts: I was thinking that our new marketing strategy needs to be more aggressive. We should focus on achieving greater visibility for the new line of laptops through advertising and better product placement in retail stores.

Mr. Daniels: That's a good point, but we don't have the budget for that.

Mr. Roberts: We need to find the budget for it. It's crucial that we get the consumers' eyes on the product while it's still cutting edge.

Mr. Daniels: I can go along with you on that, but we simply don't have the money.

Mr. Roberts: What if we could find the money by reallocating funds from promoting some of our more established products?

Mr. Daniels: That might work.

Mr. Roberts: Great. I'll contact accounting to get an idea of the money we have available.

Mr. Daniels: Let me recap what we discussed earlier. Mr. Roberts, you are going to write out a proposal for the new campaign by Tuesday and send it to me. When do you think you can finish that budget data?

Mr. Roberts: I'll try to get it by tomorrow.

Mr. Daniels: Okay. I think that's it for today. Keep me posted about your progress.

Questions

1. What approach does Mr. Roberts want to take?
2. Why does Mr. Daniels oppose Mr. Roberts's idea?
3. In your culture, is it easy to make a stance to your boss? Why or why not?

3 LANGUAGE FOCUS

••• KEY PATTERNS

Here are some key patterns that you can use when persuading others to your side.

Let me recap...
- what we discussed in the meeting.
- what we decided last time.
- the research that our team compiled.

That's a good point, but...
- you have to consider things from our point of view.
- our research disagrees.
- the latest data disproves that approach.

I can go along with...
- your plan if you meet me halfway.
- what you are asking.
- your demands.

4 SET THE STAGE

CASE SCENARIOS

Read each scenario and complete each stage.

1 Business Expressions

Read the expressions and write your own sentence using each expression.

think on your feet react to events effectively, without prior thought or planning.
Ex) You can really think on your feet. I would have had no idea of what to do in that situation.
Sentence
_____

ways and means the methods and resources for achieving something
Ex) Our team is looking into the ways and means of exporting the new product line.
Sentence
_____

keep an eye on to keep under careful observation
Ex) We need to keep an eye on the situation before entering into an agreement.
Sentence
_____

Scenario #1

 Team Member (Wants to keep current supplier)
 Manager (Wants to change to a cheaper supplier)

Your team has been asked to write a report detailing your company's wholesale supplier options for product components. Your manager thinks that your company should change to a cheaper supplier. You think that the difference in price is too small to risk ruining your company's long-term relationship with your current supplier. Persuade your co-worker over to your side.

Stage 1. Brainstorm the mission of each character.
_____
_____

Stage 2. Role play.
Be sure to complete the mission of each character and use at least 2 key patterns.

Scenario #2

 Team Member 1 (Taking notes)
 Team Member 2 (Presenting personal goals)

You are responsible for taking notes about individual sales goals in your team's monthly sales meeting. Listen to your co-worker's goals. Repeat the information that you heard and listen carefully as your co-worker clarifies a few points.

Stage 1. Brainstorm the mission of each character.
_____
_____

Stage 2. Role play.
Be sure to complete the mission of each character and use at least 2 key patterns

5 BUSINESS BASICS

FUN FACTS

Did you know?

❶ Cambodia held a national election in July 2003, but it took one year of negotiations between political parties before a coalition government was formed.

❷ Australia and East Timor have had ongoing negotiations about their maritime boundary since 2002.

Taking a Position

Business is about making deals. As Harvard Business professor, James K. Sebenius says, "Wherever parties with different interests and perceptions depend on each other for results, negotiation matters." Companies need to hone deal-making and negotiation skills as a core competency and talent throughout their workforce, especially in those responsible for making contracts.

Every negotiation can be reduced down to two choices: making the deal and the best no-deal option. In other words, if one party does not make the deal, what action will that party take? Your quest is to make a deal and communicate effectively how your deal is better than that competing no-deal option. Also, to close the deal, you must put yourself in the other side's shoes and solve their problem.

Closing the Deal : Getting it done	
Skill	**Effect**
Cultural Intelligence / Cross-Cultural Negotiation	Showing knowledge and appreciation of the cultural mindset
	Creating a bigger win for each side; a bigger "pie"
	Creating a sense of loss and paranoia if the deal does not happen
	Bringing together a few issues to make a more comprehensive and total deal
	Catering to your individual needs and nuances

Share Your Thoughts

1. Read the effects and match the correct skills. Which skill do you think is most valuable in closing deals?

   *Increase the 'pie' / Create Fear / Overcome Stereotypes
   Combine Issues : Packages Deals*

2. Narrow vs. Broad. In negotiation, the point is to reach a deal. Which do you think is more effective: focusing and agreeing on specific details or getting a broad agreement?

3. Some lawyers say that your side should always be the one to propose the contract and that you should never sign a contract proposed by the other side. Do you agree?

6 NUMBERS & FACTS

Cultural Note

In New Zealand, France, Germany, and Poland, all take offense at the chewing of gum in public.

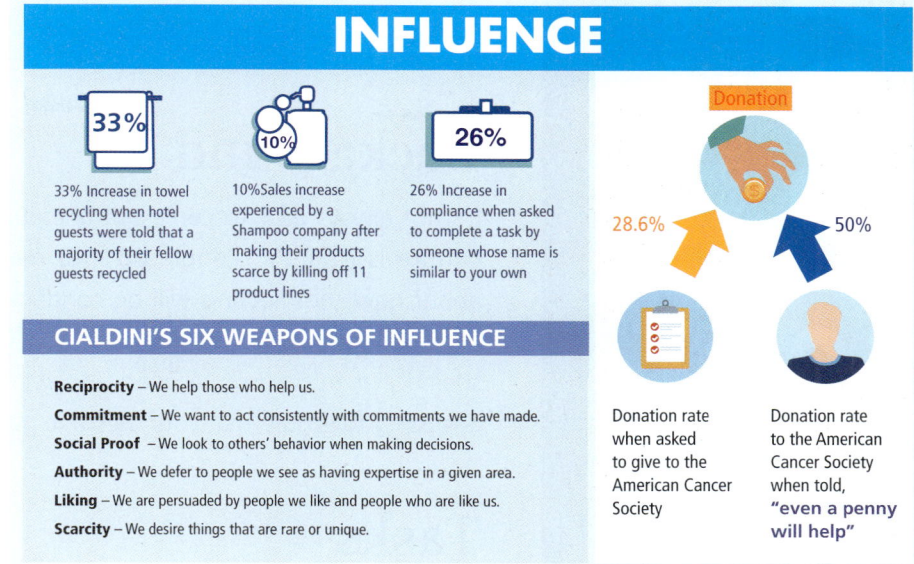

Look at the image above to answer the following questions.

1. How much does compliance to a task increase when the asker has a name similar to your own?

2. Summarize the data given about American Cancer Society donations. Why do you think the "even a penny will help" slogan is more persuasive than simply asking?

3. Read through Cialdini's Six Weapons of Influence. Are there any points that you disagree with based on your personal experience?
Think of another "weapon" to add to the list.

Share 3 new things you learned from this lesson:

1.

2.

3.

7 REVIEW & PREVIEW

Sneak Peek

1. How do you view humor in a business environment? When is it appropriate or inappropriate? Have you ever used humor effectively in business such as to make a new contact during networking or to change a negative situation into a good situation?

2. How much do you think being a good socializer is a part of business success? Do you think some people get further in their careers due to being smooth with words?

CASE STUDY
Cross-cultural Negotiations Strategies and Preparations

Background

It's not always easy to come out ahead in a negotiation — especially when culture is a factor. People go into meetings with a lot of assumptions about how the meeting will be conducted and what can go unsaid. When negotiating in a multi-cultural setting, these assumptions are not always shared. For this reason, a good understanding of the other party's culture is necessary to ensure that your message gets across clearly.

Tasks

01 Imagine you are on a team that is opening negotiations with a Saudi Arabian company. Consider the following cultural factors and compare them to business practices in your own country. Brainstorm a strategy to prepare yourself for similar behavior.

Factor	Saudi Arabia	Your Country	Possible Strategy
Punctuality	Time is very flexible. Meetings may start very late (if at all) and last for hours.		
Behavior	Speaking in a loud and aggressive manner shows engagement and interest - not anger or hostility.		
Hierarchy	Saudis dislike negotiating with someone who has to get approval from a higher up and can interpret this as disrespect toward them.		
Relationships	It is necessary to get to know each other personally before working together, so business might not even be discussed in a first meeting.		
Saving Face	The boss is usually considered right no matter what, so who says something is often more important than what is said.		

UNIT 2.
Winning Negotiator

02
Compare what you wrote with your partner. Were your ideas similar?

03
You are working for Garcant, Inc., an international construction company, that is finalizing its negotiations with a Saudia Arabian company to build an oil refinery. The scale of the project is very large, so you want to make sure that this negotiation is a win-win without compromising your company's needs. Meet with one of the company's representatives and work out the final details of the contract.
Write down the terms that you agree on.

Decisions	Student A: **Garcant, Inc.**	Student B: **Saudia Arabian Side**
Start Date	4 months later	2 months later
Estimated Completion Time	2 years	20 months
Cost	$2.5 billion (materials cost flexible)	$2.5 billion (including all materials)
Workforce	local for labor, engineers and mangagement from your country	local for labor, engineers and mangagement (40% local, 60% Garcant, Inc.)

Decisions	Final Agreement
Start Date	
Estimated Completion Time	
Cost	
Workforce	

LESSON 09

UNIT 3. POSITIVE INTERACTION

Using Humor

Overview

- [ ] Getting Started
- [ ] Situational Dialogue
- [ ] Language Focus
- [ ] Set the Stage
- [ ] Business Basics
- [ ] Numbers and Facts

[Learning Objectives] Upon completion of this lesson, you will be able to…
- ease a tense situation through witty comments
- recognize different types of witty comments and show humor

1 GETTING STARTED

1 Warm up

Let's open the floor. What are your opinions?

01.
What are some ways that you can ease uncomfortable situations? Why is this important?

02.
Do you feel that you have a witty personality? Explain.

03.
How important is a good sense of humor in your country's business culture? Why do you feel this way?

2 Formal vs. Informal

Write the correct phrases in the formal or informal column of the table according to the tone.

a. It's going to be fine.
b. No worries.
c. Relax.
d. You earned it!
e. Stop worrying.
f. My mistake.
g. That's too bad.
h. Don't stress yourself out.
i. It's not that big of an issue.
j. Everything is going to be fine.
k. I'm sincerely sorry to hear that.
l. It was completely my fault.
m. You will do better next time.
n. No one deserves this more than you.
o. There is nothing to worry about.
p. Don't come in late again.
q. Please try to calm yourself.
r. Please remember to proof-read the report before you send it.

Function	Formal	Informal
Easing tension		
Offering encouragement		
Alleviating worry		
Offering sympathy		
Accepting blame		
Warning		
Reassuring		
Downplaying a mistake		
Congratulating		

2 SITUATIONAL DIALOGUE

1 Before reading the dialogue, use the information given below to answer the following questions.

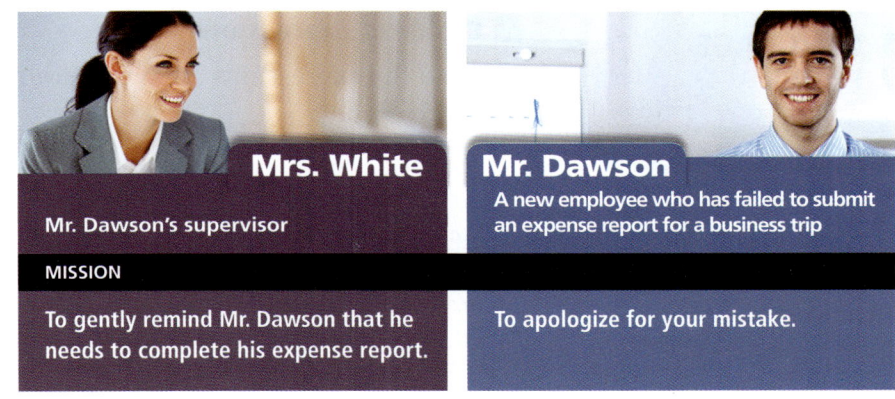

Mrs. White — Mr. Dawson's supervisor
MISSION: To gently remind Mr. Dawson that he needs to complete his expense report.

Mr. Dawson — A new employee who has failed to submit an expense report for a business trip
To apologize for your mistake.

1. Look at the characters and describe the situation.
2. What is the relationship between the characters?
3. What do you think will happen next?

2 Practice the dialogue and answer the comprehension questions.

Giving a Gentle Warning

Mrs. White: I still haven't gotten your expense report from the last business trip. You know what they say better late than never, but better never late!

Mr. Dawson: I'm sorry about that. I've just been a little overwhelmed with work.

Mrs. White: That's understandable, but you should get that in soon. Accounting has been asking. You better make sure it's flawless really dot your i's and cross your t's.

Mr. Dawson: Yes, of course.

Mrs. White: Corporate is kind of picky about having documentation for things charged on the company card. We did get a lot of free meals out of this trip, so you've got to put in the proper documentation.

Mr. Dawson: I guess it's a small price to pay.

Mrs. White: Yeah. You can't have your cake and eat it, too.

Mr. Dawson: Okay. I'm sorry again about the delay. I'll try to be more punctual from now on.

Mrs. White: That's okay. Just don't let it happen again.

Mr. Dawson: I'm going to go get started on it right now. Thanks for reminding me.

Questions

1. What are some advantages of using witty comments to make messages less direct? Explain.
2. How could Mrs. White have phrased her warning more directly?
3. Do you prefer to receive criticism directly or gently? Why?

Lesson 9. Using Humor

3 LANGUAGE FOCUS

••• KEY PATTERNS

Here are some key patterns that you can use when making witty comments.

Better late than never, but better never late!
- We need to hurry up.
- Aren't you finished yet?
- You know what they say.

dot your i's and cross your t's
- Don't forget to…
- You need to really… for this client.
- Make sure to…

You can't have your cake and eat it, too
- Don't worry so much.
- Don't show up late if you want to get a promotion.
- It's not that big of a problem.

4 SET THE STAGE

CASE SCENARIOS

Read each scenario and complete each stage.

1 Business Expressions

Read the expressions and write your own sentence using each expression.

sooner or later at some time in the future; eventually
Ex) Don't worry about success now. I'm sure you'll find it sooner or later.
Sentence

work down to the wire to work until the very last moment possible
Ex) I can't believe we're so behind on this project. We'll have to work down to the wire to finish.
Sentence

read somebody's mind to guess what someone is thinking; to share a similar opinion
Ex) That's exactly what I was thinking! It's like you read my mind.
Sentence

Scenario #1  Role A: Supervisor   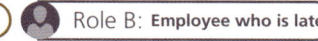 Role B: Employee who is late

A new employee is late to his or her first day of work due to traffic. Listen to the employee apologize and explain the situation. Assure the new employee that everything is fine and make him or her comfortable with a witty remark.

Stage 1. Brainstorm the mission of each character.

Stage 2. Role play.
Be sure to complete the mission of each character and use at least 2 key patterns.

Scenario #2  Role A: Team Leader   Role B: Subordinate

You are a Team Leader in the Sales Department. One of your team members has been assigned to an important new client. Before he or she leaves for a meeting, remind the team member of how serious the situation is and ask him or her to be careful. Use wit to ensure they do not leave feeling too tense.

Stage 1. Brainstorm the mission of each character.

Stage 2. Role play.
Be sure to complete the mission of each character and use at least 2 key patterns.

5 BUSINESS BASICS

Being witty can be a great way to enliven your conversation. Not only will you be memorable, but most likely you will have added some cheer to others. Having wit is not about showing off but about showing connections between the nature of things.

Being funny is not necessarily a mystery. Comedians who make jokes for a living are able to explain the basics of how comedy and wittiness works. Here a few basic components of being funny.

Comedic Skills		
Tactic	**Method**	**Situation**
Funny Word Choice	Sometimes pick an unusual word to exaggerate a characteristic of something.	
Reduction	Make things smaller than usual.	
Inflation	Make things bigger than usual.	
Mismatch	Juxtapose or combine things that do not usually go together.	
Surprise	Create an expectation and deliver the opposite.	

FUN FACTS

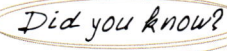

❶ Laughter is contagious. The sound of laughter will often trigger more laughter. The Tanganyikan (Tanzania and Uganda) laughter epidemic immobilized an entire school district during 1962.

❷ Laughing 100 times has the same effect on the body as being on a rowing machine for 10 minutes or riding an exercise bike for 15 minutes.

Share Your Thoughts

1. Fill in the table above with a situation in which the comedic tactic would be appropriate. Which comedic tactic is easiest for you?

2. Do you think that some people take wittiness too far? How would you deal with a co-worker whom you think jokes too much?

3. If you were giving a presentation or speech, would you try to use comedy? If so, how would you incorporate it? Where would you put it: beginning, middle, end, or spontaneously?

6 NUMBERS & FACTS

Cultural Note

In the Philippines, to eat everything on your plate is considered rude, whereas **in Finland,** to leave food on your plate is rude.

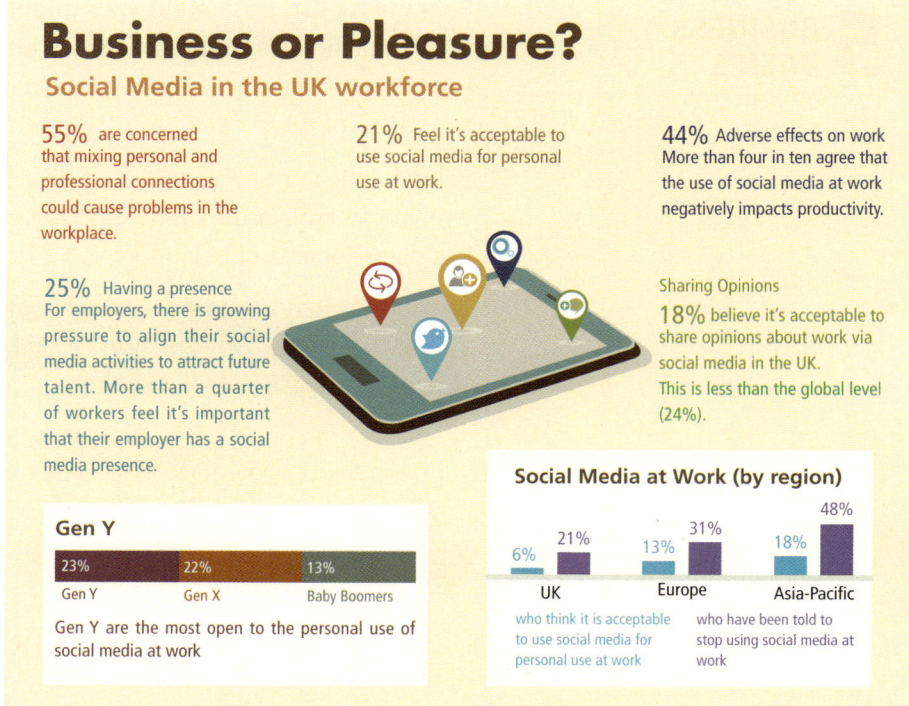

Business or Pleasure?
Social Media in the UK workforce

55% are concerned that mixing personal and professional connections could cause problems in the workplace.

21% Feel it's acceptable to use social media for personal use at work.

44% Adverse effects on work More than four in ten agree that the use of social media at work negatively impacts productivity.

25% Having a presence For employers, there is growing pressure to align their social media activities to attract future talent. More than a quarter of workers feel it's important that their employer has a social media presence.

Sharing Opinions
18% believe it's acceptable to share opinions about work via social media in the UK.
This is less than the global level (24%).

Gen Y
23% Gen Y | 22% Gen X | 13% Baby Boomers
Gen Y are the most open to the personal use of social media at work

Social Media at Work (by region)
UK: 6% / 21%
Europe: 13% / 31%
Asia-Pacific: 18% / 48%

who think it is acceptable to use social media for personal use at work
who have been told to stop using social media at work

Look at the image above to answer the following questions.

1. Which region has the most prevalent workplace social media use? What percentage of employees are allowed to use social media at work?

2. What percentage of workers feel that it is important for their employer to have an online presence? Do you agree or disagree?

3. Globally, 24% of people believe that it is acceptable to share opinions about work via social media. Do you feel that this is professional? Explain. Is there any information that should never be shared?

7 REVIEW & PREVIEW

Share 3 new things you learned from this lesson:

1.

2.

3.

 **Sneak Peek**

1. Do you think it is difficult to change another person's mind? Is it difficult for someone to change your mind? Please explain your answers.

2. Which do you consider more effective for framing an argument: numbers/data or emotions?

LESSON

10

UNIT 3. POSITIVE INTERACTION

Turning the Table

Overview

- [ ] Getting Started
- [ ] Situational Dialogue
- [ ] Language Focus
- [ ] Set the Stage
- [ ] Business Basics
- [ ] Numbers and Facts

[Learning Objectives] Upon completion of this lesson, you will be able to...
- use strategies to turn the business situation to your advantage
- persuade others with evidence and supporting details

1 GETTING STARTED

1 Warm up

Let's open the floor. What are your opinions?

01.
How can you maintain a positive atmosphere in negotiations? Explain.

02.
What are some ways to provide evidence to support your points? Give examples.

03.
Describe an experience where you persuaded someone.
How did you do it?

2 Formal vs. Informal

Write the correct phrases in the formal or informal column of the table according to the tone.

a. See you next time.
b. I think that is wrong.
c. I can see your point.
d. Thank you for your time.
e. Disney is a great example of this.
f. Fine, if you sign the contract.
g. I don't agree with your point.
h. Your argument has convinced me.
i. I think we need a new sales strategy.
j. Check out this marketing survey.
k. I would happily agree if you increase your order by 3%.
l. Also, this strategy would make us more money.
m. Do you have any more info about that?
n. Furthermore, increasing advertising would yield more revenue.
o. Could you please elaborate on that statement?
p. In my opinion, this is the best course of action.
q. Consider the example of Apple's marketing strategy.
r. Please consider the results of the 2014 clinical trial.

Function	Formal	Informal
Providing evidence		
Asking for more information		
Disagreeing		
Highlighting an example		
Continuing an argument		
Stating an opinion		
Offering a condition		
Conceding		
Closing a meeting		

Lesson 10. Turning the Table

2 SITUATIONAL DIALOGUE

1 Before reading the dialogue, use the information given below to answer the following questions.

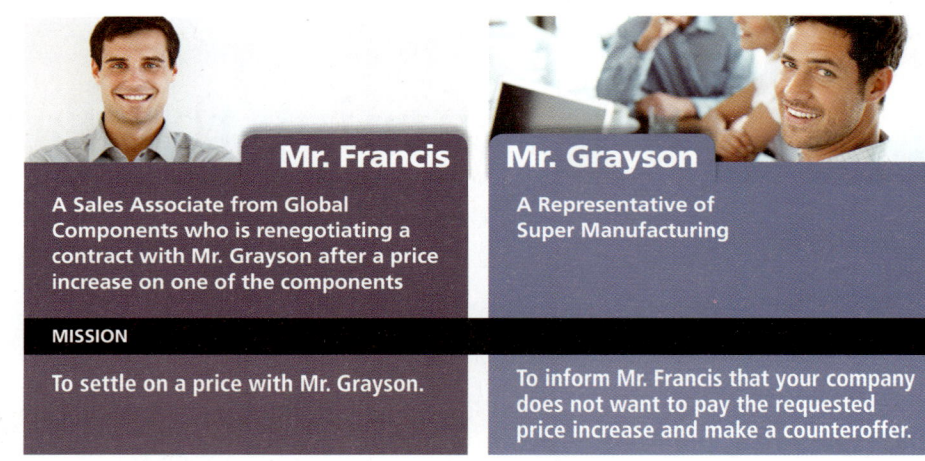

Mr. Francis
A Sales Associate from Global Components who is renegotiating a contract with Mr. Grayson after a price increase on one of the components

MISSION
To settle on a price with Mr. Grayson.

Mr. Grayson
A Representative of Super Manufacturing

To inform Mr. Francis that your company does not want to pay the requested price increase and make a counteroffer.

1. Look at the characters and describe the situation
2. What is the relationship between the characters?
3. What do you think will happen next?

2 Practice the dialogue and answer the comprehension questions.

Final Compromise

Mr. Francis: Thank you for meeting me here today, Mr. Grayson. I hope you've given what we discussed last time some consideration.

Mr. Grayson: Yes, I discussed it with my partners, and I'd be willing to comply if you met us on a few points. According to our finance team, it seems that we can't quite afford the price increase that you are suggesting. We can offer you 8% more, but that's the best we can do.

Mr. Francis: I'm sorry, but I see no choice but to refuse that offer.

Mr. Grayson: What if we agree to purchase a larger volume? We are one of your company's largest customers, so an increase of that much could yield substantial profits.

Mr. Francis: That might be an option. Could you be more specific about the volume?

Mr. Grayson: We are prepared to increase our purchasing by 5%.

Mr. Francis: Is there anything else you want to add?

Mr. Grayson: No, I think that addresses everything.

Mr. Francis: Okay. I'm not authorized to discount the price that much, but I will be happy to check with my supervisor. I'll just go ask him now and get you your answer.

Mr. Grayson: Thank you very much.

Questions

1. What did Mr. Grayson offer? How did he try to persuade Mr. Francis?

2. Do you think compromise is easy to achieve in your country's business culture? Why or why not?

3. What advice would you give someone looking to improve their persuasive skills? Explain.

3 LANGUAGE FOCUS

••• KEY PATTERNS

Here are some key patterns that you can use when trying to turn the table on a situation.

I see no choice but to...
- change our approach.
- reevaluate our goals.
- start again from scratch.

According to... , it seems that...
- the client…they are interested in a change.
- the data…we need to change our strategy.
- George…a lot of progress has been made.

I'd be willing to comply if you...
- met me halfway.
- agreed with me on this point.
- found more evidence to support your idea.

4 SET THE STAGE

CASE SCENARIOS

Read each scenario and complete each stage.

1 Business Expressions

Read the expressions and write your own sentence using each expression.

know something inside out understand something very thoroughly
Ex) We're really lucky to have Bob on our team. He really knows his stuff inside out.
Sentence

easier said than done be more easily talked about than put into practice
Ex) Achieving a goal is something easier said than done.
Sentence

to stay on top of things to remain in control of a situation
Ex) We're dealing with an important client, so we really need to stay on top of things.
Sentence

Scenario #1

 Role A: Employee (Favors a new sales approach)
 Role B: Supervisor (Wants to stay with the current approach)

You are employed in the Sales Department of a pharmaceutical company. Your team has come up with a new sales strategy for a recently released blood pressure drug. You propose the idea to your supervisor, but he thinks that it is best to continue with the current strategy. Persuade your boss to your side by describing research that has been done about the market for the drug.

Stage 1. Brainstorm the mission of each character.

Stage 2. Role play.
Be sure to complete the mission of each character and use at least 2 key patterns.

Scenario #2

Role A: Sales Associate from Star Enterprises
Role B: Representative from Kayu, Inc.

You are responsible for negotiating a new contract with one of your company's suppliers. The company has said that they cannot go any lower on the price, but you have a feeling that you can get them to go lower if you agree to sign a long-term contract. Ask questions to confirm your hypothesis and make your offer.

Stage 1. Brainstorm the mission of each character.

Stage 2. Role play.
Be sure to complete the mission of each character and use at least 2 key patterns.

Lesson 10. Turning the Table

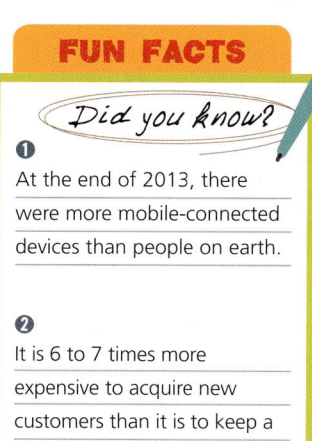

FUN FACTS

Did you know?

❶ At the end of 2013, there were more mobile-connected devices than people on earth.

❷ It is 6 to 7 times more expensive to acquire new customers than it is to keep a current one.

Turning the Table

When making a proposition or entering a negotiation, it is common to find yourself facing opposition. When you find yourself in a situation where people attack or resist your ideas, you should try your best to frame the discussion in a positive way. Also, a key aspect is to establish rapport with the audience and even the opposition, whenever possible. Using terms of respect in address and setting a positive agenda can create a matrix for discussion in your favor.

Overcoming opposition could involve many layers and phases. For example, before you even begin advocating your position, you should get to know the other side as deeply as possible.

Turning the Table : Skill Set	
Skill	**Value**
	"Ethos" is the audience's perception of you, be authentic! Create expertise, so people trust you more.
	You can recognize criticism but reframe it in a way so that it loses its potency.
	Show how something supposedly negative is actually positive.
	Humans often trust their eyes more than other senses such as logical reasoning.
	Connect to humans deeply and emotionally through a narrative in which they can participate and invest.
	Set up a parallel story or example so that the lessons from that example transfer to your position.
	Questioning the other side also works. Create doubt.

Share Your Thoughts

1. Read the given values and match each with the correct skill.
   Add your own skills and explain.

   > Question / Create a positive 'ethos' / Rephrase / Tell a story
   > Use analogy / Compelling visuals / Admit but re-evaluate

2. If someone accused your idea of betraying the company values, how would you respond?

3. Sometimes people judge the "vessel" and not the contents.
   How would you respond if people negatively judged you according to your appearance or position?

6 NUMBERS & FACTS

Cultural Note

In the country of Georgia, little children might pinch the skin of the front of their throat and pull it outwards. This gesture is a sign of humble request, saying "please."

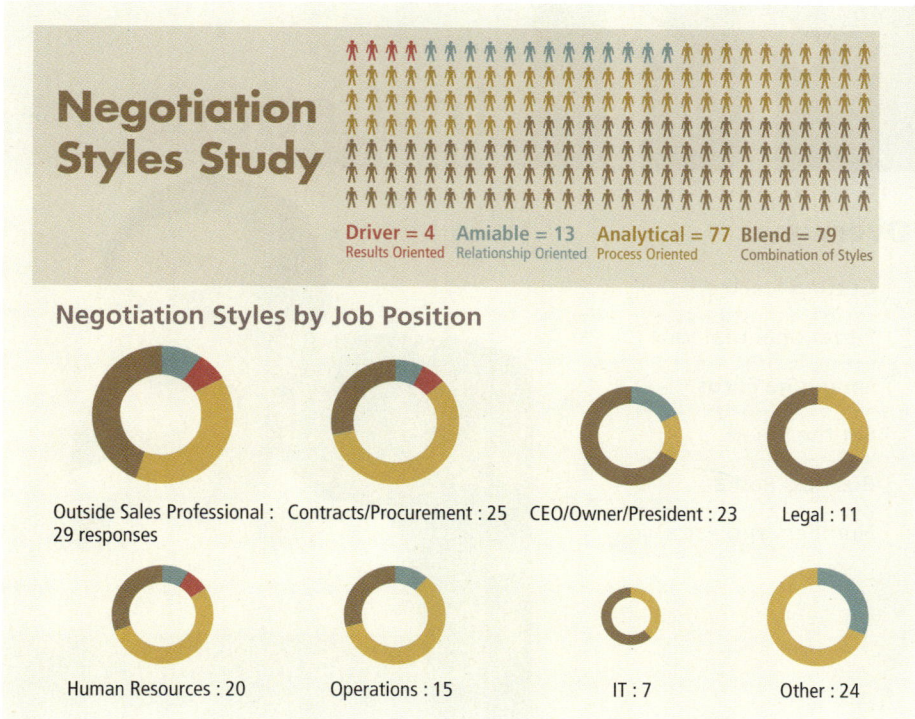

Look at the image above to answer the following questions.

1. How many people in Contracts/Procurement job positions were surveyed? What was the most common negotiation style among these participants?

2. Only 4 out of 173 participants described themselves as a "driver" or "results oriented" negotiator. Why do you think this is?

3. Which job positions favored analytical negotiation styles? Why do you think this is?

7 REVIEW & PREVIEW

Share 3 new things you learned from this lesson:

1.

2.

3.

 Sneak Peek

1. When you invite someone out for a dinner, what is your typical custom? Do you have a certain number of days in advance by which you make the invitation?

2. Do you think making a reservation creates a good impression? How do you feel about making or accepting business dinner reservations?

LESSON 11

UNIT 3. POSITIVE INTERACTION

Invitations

Overview

- [ ] Getting Started
- [ ] Situational Dialogue
- [ ] Language Focus
- [ ] Set the Stage
- [ ] Business Basics
- [ ] Numbers and Facts

[Learning Objectives] Upon completion of this lesson, you will be able to…
- cordially invite people out for meals
- make reservations at a restaurant

1 GETTING STARTED

1 Warm up

Let's open the floor. What are your opinions?

01.
Do you often have to eat meals with business partners?
How do you bring up the subject?

02.
What are some questions you should ask someone when making plans to eat together? What type of dietary restrictions might they have?

03.
What type of food would you recommend to a foreign visitor to your country? Explain your choice.

2 Formal vs. Informal

Write the correct phrases in the formal or informal column of the table according to the tone.

a. Sorry, but I'm busy.
b. How about around 3:00?
c. What's kosher?
d. Any plans for tonight?
e. Do you enjoy Thai food?
f. Sounds like a plan.
g. How about Chinese?
h. What's good around here?
i. Do you have any vegetarian options?
j. Make me a reservation for 7:00.
k. Do you have anything planned for next Tuesday?
l. Do you have any tables available at 9:00 tonight?
m. I'd be delighted to join you.
n. I'm sorry, but I have a schedule conflict.
o. Would it be possible to meet at 6:00?
p. Could you recommend a good restaurant in the area?
q. You should try Golden Palace if you enjoy Chinese.
r. The Mill Street Grill is the best.

Function	Formal	Informal
Setting a time		
Asking about food preferences		
Inquiring about schedules		
Accepting an invitation		
Refusing an invitation		
Asking for a suggestion		
Offering a recommendation		
Making a reservation		
Discussing dietary restrictions		

2 SITUATIONAL DIALOGUE

1 Before reading the dialogue, use the information given below to answer the following questions.

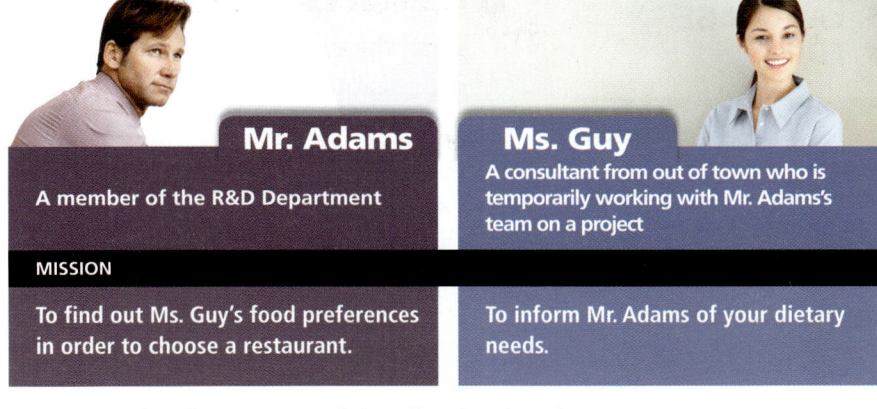

Mr. Adams — A member of the R&D Department

Ms. Guy — A consultant from out of town who is temporarily working with Mr. Adams's team on a project

MISSION

To find out Ms. Guy's food preferences in order to choose a restaurant.

To inform Mr. Adams of your dietary needs.

1. Look at the characters and describe the situation.
2. What is the relationship between the characters?
3. What do you think will happen next?

2 Practice the dialogue and answer the comprehension questions.

Dinner Invitation

Mr. Adams: It's been a pleasure getting to know you today, Ms. Guy. If you have some time, would you like to join my team for dinner tonight?

Ms. Guy: That would be great. I don't really know anyone here, so I really appreciate the invitation.

Mr. Adams: Wonderful! What would you like to eat? There are a lot of good restaurants that we could go to.

Ms. Guy: What would you recommend for a vegetarian?

Mr. Adams: I know a couple of places. Do you prefer Indian or French?

Ms. Guy: Indian would be nice.

Mr. Adams: Okay. I'll let the team know. I can pick you up at your hotel. When's a good time to stop by?

Ms. Guy: How about around 7:00?

Mr. Adams: Perfect. I'll give you a call when I'm almost there.

Ms. Guy: Okay. Great. See you soon.

Questions

1. What do you think Mr. Adams and Ms. Guy will do following the conversation?
2. In your country, do you often eat with co-workers and business partners? Explain.
3. What would you recommend for a vegetarian to eat in your country?

Lesson 11. Invitations

3 LANGUAGE FOCUS

••• KEY PATTERNS

Here are some key patterns that you can use when inviting people and making restaurant reservations.

When's a good time to...
- come by your office?
- call you to make plans?
- meet for dinner?

Do you prefer... or...
- coffee…tea?
- meeting for lunch…dinner?
- Chinese…Italian for dinner?

What would you recommend for...
- a vegan?
- someone unfamiliar with Indian food?
- someone with a peanut allergy?

1 Business Expressions

Read the expressions and write your own sentence using each expression.

get back into swing of things to return to the usual way that something is done
Ex) You only missed the first meeting. I'm sure you will get back into the swing of things soon.
Sentence _____

tough break a bit of bad luck
Ex) I'm sorry the client didn't like your proposal. That's a tough break.
Sentence _____

talk someone into something to persuade someone to adopt a certain position, belief, or course of action
Ex) It wasn't difficult to talk him into taking a vacation.
Sentence _____

4 SET THE STAGE

CASE SCENARIOS

Read each scenario and complete each stage.

Scenario #1

Role A: **Sales Representative**
Role B: **Restaurant Employee**

You are planning to take one of your company's clients out for dinner. Call to make a reservation. The restaurant has several menu options that must be reserved in advance. Agree on a time and ask about which options are suitable for your client's needs.

Stage 1. Brainstorm the mission of each character.
_____
_____

Stage 2. Role play.
Be sure to complete the mission of each character and use at least 2 key patterns.

Scenario #2

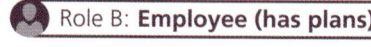
Role A: **Supervisor (wants to go out to dinner)**
Role B: **Employee (has plans)**

You want to take one of your team members out for dinner to reward him or her for closing a big deal. The team member has a busy schedule and the first three times you ask they have other plans. Let the team member set the date and time and agree upon a restaurant.

Stage 1. Brainstorm the mission of each character.
_____
_____

Stage 2. Role play.
Be sure to complete the mission of each character and use at least 2 key patterns.

5 BUSINESS BASICS

Invitations

Invitations are very intimate decisions because they are directed at a specific group of guests who have been selected by the host. Also, the manner of extending the invitation sets the tone of the encounter. Likewise, the set (who is invited) and the setting (location) establishes the level of decorum. Dealing with invitations properly gets everything started on the right note. Promptness and clarity are the best qualities on each side.

Invitations are the act of inviting. Below are some signifiers of the two main categories of invitations. However, in both cases, the invitations should include all the necessary information.

Informal
- Invitation face-to-face or via e-mail, text, or phone call
- Guests take care of their own arrival
- Basic table setting or limited service
- Random seating arrangement
- Split the tab
  Each person pays separately

Formal
- RSVP card sent by mail
  Response card included
- Possibly escort your guests by picking them up or offering a parking voucher
- More elaborate table setting
  Possibly a few courses of food served
- Name cards to designate seating
- The host serves and pays in full

FUN FACTS

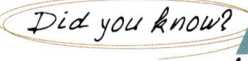

❶ Nearly 98% of Indians prefer face-to-face interaction with business contacts while carrying out a deal, says a survey by global telecom firm Cable and Wireless Worldwide.

❷ Gen Y will form 75% of the workforce by 2025 and are actively shaping corporate culture and expectations. Only 11% say that earning a lot of money is a definition of success.

Share Your Thoughts

1. Please give examples of occasions when you would use the informal or formal style. Are there any situations where both are suitable?

2. If you were a guest and your host committed an etiquette error, how would you respond?

3. Nowadays some people use online services such as e-vites to send electronic invitations via e-mail. How do you feel about this form of invitation?

6 NUMBERS & FACTS

Cultural Note

Importing and/or wearing military clothing *in Guatemala* (Central America) is illegal. Also, sadly enough, kidnappings occur, so photographing children is very inappropriate.

Look at the image above to answer the following questions.

1. How much was Google able to decrease employees' caloric consumption by placing candy in opaque bins?

2. Explain the green and red food tags at Google. How might this help improve employees' eating habits?

3. What do you think the purpose of Google's People Analytics department is? How could a program like this be applied in your own workplace? Explain.

Share 3 new things you learned from this lesson:

1.

2.

3.

7 REVIEW & PREVIEW

 Sneak Peek

1. Are you aware of any culturally inappropriate compliments? Are there some compliments in your culture or country that bother you?

2. Does your company have any special routines for the workers to get to know each other?

LESSON 12

UNIT 3. POSITIVE INTERACTION

Maintaining Positive Relationships

Overview

- [ ] Getting Started
- [ ] Situational Dialogue
- [ ] Language Focus
- [ ] Set the Stage
- [ ] Business Basics
- [ ] Numbers and Facts

[Learning Objectives] Upon completion of this lesson, you will be able to…
- use various methods to compliment others
- recognize different ways to maintain and establish positive relationships in the workplace

1 GETTING STARTED

1 Warm up

Let's open the floor. What are your opinions?

01.
What are some ways that you can create a positive working environment? Explain.

02.
Do you think compliments are valuable in the workplace? Why or why not?

03.
What social tips would you give to a foreigner working in an office in your country?

2 Formal vs. Informal

Write the correct phrases in the formal or informal column of the table according to the tone.

a. Looking good today!
b. Thanks for that.
c. Need a hand?
d. Good luck!
e. Want something to drink?
f. Thank you, I really appreciate it.
g. What's up?
h. It was all thanks to my team.
i. How was your weekend?
j. How do you get your hair to look so nice?
k. Great work on the Fairmont report.
l. What's your secret for dealing with difficult clients?
m. Mr. Johnson deserves the credit for this achievement.
n. Your new hair style really suits you.
o. Your progress on the Italian project is admirable.
p. Would you like some help with that?
q. I hope your presentation goes well.
r. Would you like some coffee while I'm up?

Function	Formal	Informal
Complimenting appearance		
Making small talk		
Acknowledging an achievement		
Giving others credit		
Accepting a compliment		
Complimenting indirectly		
Offering a drink		
Offering assistance		
Wishing luck		

Lesson 12. Maintaining Positive Relationships

2 SITUATIONAL DIALOGUE

1 Before reading the dialogue, use the information given below to answer the following questions.

Ms. Masters — Mr. Miles's Supervisor
MISSION: To ask Mr. Miles to lead the company's presentation skills seminar while complimenting his work

Mr. Miles — A member of the Sales Department
To further his career opportunities by using his strength in presentations to gain experience

1. Look at the characters and describe the situation
2. What is the relationship between the characters?
3. What do you think will happen next?

2 Practice the dialogue and answer the comprehension questions.

Boss's Compliment

Ms. Masters: Good morning, Mr. Miles. You look well today.

Mr. Miles: Thank you. How are you?

Ms. Masters: I'm fine. I just wanted to say that we were all really impressed with your presentation yesterday.

Mr. Miles: Thank you for saying that. It means a lot coming from you.

Ms. Masters: What's your secret for staying so energetic? You gave such a convincing argument for the clients.

Mr. Miles: I guess I just really believed what I was saying.

Ms. Masters: Anyway, I think you have great presentation skills and that you would be an excellent person to lead our presentation skills seminar for new hires.

Mr. Miles: Really? I would be interested in doing that.

Ms. Masters: That's good to hear. I'll let you know the details later.

Mr. Miles: Thank you for considering me.

Questions

1. Why did Ms. Masters begin the conversation by complimenting Mr. Miles?
2. Are you comfortable receiving compliments? How do people respond to compliments in your culture?
3. How did Ms. Masters give compliments in the dialogue? What other ways do you know to give compliments?

3 LANGUAGE FOCUS

••• KEY PATTERNS

Here are some key patterns that you can use when maintaining and establishing positive relationships in the workplace.

You look... today.
- busy
- very handsome
- well-rested

What's your secret for...
- managing your time?
- staying fit?
- organizing your desk?

I think you have great...
- time management skills.
- ideas for the upcoming project.
- people skills.

1 Business Expressions

Read the expressions and write your own sentence using each expression.

breathe down someone's neck to follow or supervise someone too closely, making him or her uncomfortable

Ex) I'm sorry to hover. I feel like I'm always breathing down your neck.
Sentence
_____

get on one's nerves to irritate or annoy someone
Ex) The new music in the elevator is really getting on my nerves. I wish they would change it back.
Sentence
_____

jump to conclusions to make an unsupported assumption
Ex) I know things look bad now, but you shouldn't jump to conclusions. We'll finish this project on time.
Sentence
_____

4 SET THE STAGE

CASE SCENARIOS

Read each scenario and complete each stage.

Scenario #1  Role A: **Co-worker 1**  Role B: **Co-worker 2**

Your co-worker has been having a hard time with work lately. One of his or her clients is causing a lot of stress. Try to start a conversation about the matter. Listen carefully to your co-worker's problem and offer your advice.

Stage 1. Brainstorm the mission of each character.
_____

Stage 2. Role play.
Be sure to complete the mission of each character and use at least 2 key patterns.

Scenario #2  Role A: **Manager**  Role B: **Team Leader**

You want to praise one of the team leaders in your department about his or her team's good performance. Thanks to your co-worker's strong leadership skills, the team has the highest quarterly sales figures in the company. Compliment the team leader and ask for tips to help improve other teams' performance.

Stage 1. Brainstorm the mission of each character.
_____

Stage 2. Role play.
Be sure to complete the mission of each character and use at least 2 key patterns.

Lesson 12. Maintaining Positive Relationships

5 BUSINESS BASICS

FUN FACTS

Did you know?

❶ Every minute more than 205 million e-mails are sent. That's approximately 5 million e-mails per second.

❷ Just to keep employment rates constant, the worldwide number of jobs will have to increase by around 600 million over a 15-year period.

Maintaining a Positive Relationship

Relationships are alive! Relationships need the right amount of care. Like many processes, the output reflects the input. Having positive relationships might be the true wealth of life. Thus, as a part of life and healthy living, we should be conscientious about what we invest into a relationship and how we steward it.

Relationships are both inwardly and outwardly directed. We need to adjust ourselves inwardly, who we are in our character. Likewise, we must attune ourselves outwardly to the other person, how we treat others and behave.

Turning the Table : Skill Set		Rate Yourself				
Skill	**Attribute/Reason**					
Invest in yourself first	Do the things in your own life first in order to be healthy. It is hard to help others if your life is disordered.	1	2	3	4	5
Be vulnerable	Don't be afraid to share about your struggles, fears, etc. It makes you more "human" so that others can relate to you.	1	2	3	4	5
Control emotions	Sometimes, people can offend each other. It is good not to trust your first impulse but focus on the long term.	1	2	3	4	5
Maintain boundaries	Each relationship has its own outline and course, e.g. co-workers, neighbors, committee members. Treat each one accordingly.	1	2	3	4	5
Don't project	Sometimes whatever is worst in us we assume is also present in others. Treat each person as a unique individual.	1	2	3	4	5
Give the benefit of the doubt	A common rule is to operate relationships according to the "most generous interpretation". Give every word and action the best possible understanding.	1	2	3	4	5
Be yourself	If you change too much to accommodate the other, then that is not a true relationship. You must be yourself to be satisfied and add true value.	1	2	3	4	5

Share Your Thoughts

1. Rate yourself for each skill (1 = Poor, 5 = Excellent).
   What are your strengths and your weaknesses? Share with your class.

2. Do you ever compliment people without really meaning it?
   Do you consider such behavior fake, or is it a necessary part of social survival?

3. Which relationships are most difficult? Pick a relationship (any kind) and explain what makes it challenging to maintain.

6 NUMBERS & FACTS

Cultural Note

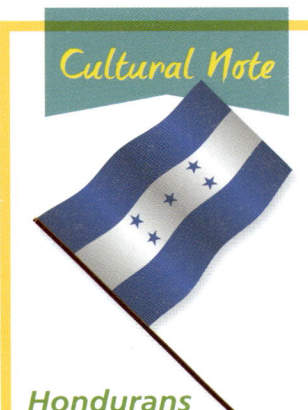

Hondurans have a peculiar way to indicate objects. They will indicate the direction of the object by tilting or turning their head, and then they will purse out their lips in a kind of "kissing" gesture.

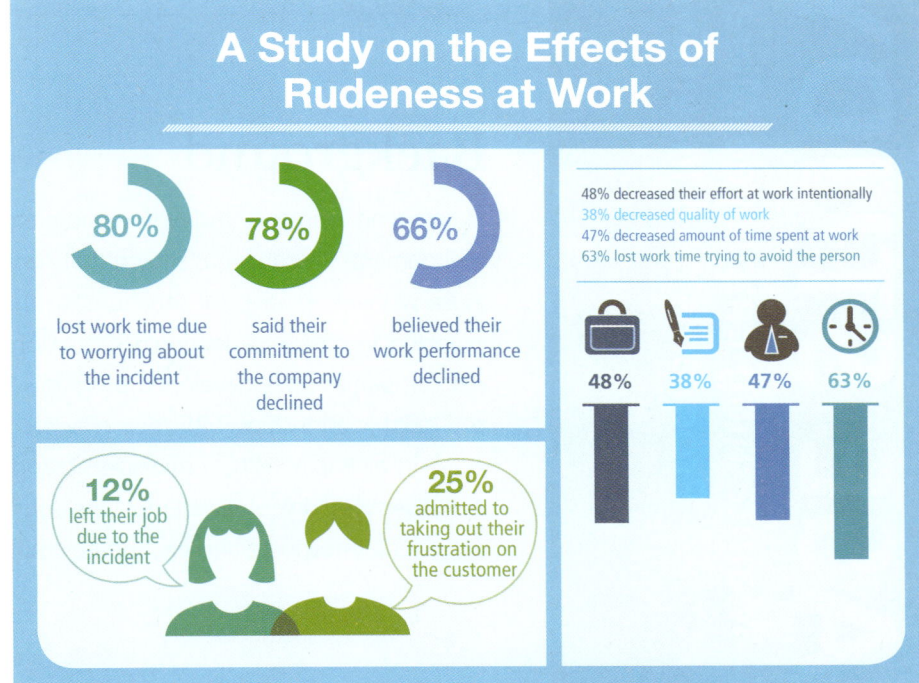

Look at the image above to answer the following questions.

1. What percentage of employees believed that their work performance declined due to an incident at work?

2. 25% of those surveyed admitted to taking out their frustration on the customer. What are some ways to relieve stress to avoid involving the customer?

3. Please use the chart to explain why rudeness in the workplace can negatively affect job performance. Do you feel that the data is reflective of your personal experiences?

Share 3 new things you learned from this lesson:

1.

2.

3.

7 REVIEW & PREVIEW

 Sneak Peek

1. Do you consider cultural awareness to be a necessary asset or just an extra feature in business relations?

2. Do you find it hard to deal with people of foreign cultures in business? Why or why not?

CASE STUDY 3
Maintaining Employee Morale Programs and Incentives

Background

Maintaining employee moral is key to creating a positive and efficient working environment. Research has shown that happy workers are more productive than those working in stressful situations. In the U.S. alone, worker unhappiness is expected to cost a staggering $300 billion in lost productivity annually. Many top companies have developed programs to help their workers alleviate stress and build relationships with their co-workers. Imagine you are an HR manager working at Rapid Tech, a mid-sized corporation. What kind of programs and incentives would you use to motivate your staff? Consider activities to improve the office atmosphere and encourage employee bonding.

Tasks

01 Rank the following ideas based on how practical they would be in your office situation. Add your own ideas to the list.

- Create employee hobby clubs
- Host fun classes and events after work or on the weekend
- Schedule group lunches, so people who don't normally interact have a change to get to know each other.
- Provide comfortable spaces for workers to interact with couches, snacks and beverages
- Host activities for employees' families at work, like picnics or holiday parties.
- Sponsor company sports teams and challenges for charity, like half marathons
- Hold work book clubs
- ?
- ?

UNIT 3.
Posit ive Interaction

02

Choose an idea to expand into an employee bonding event.

	What	
	Who	
	When	
	Where	
?	Things to Prepare	

03

Write an e-mail inviting people to the event.

_____
_____
_____
_____
_____
_____

04

Consider your own workplace. What kind of incentives would be most motivating to you and your co-workers?

1. *Extra vacation days*
2.
3.
4.
5.
6.
7.
8.
9.
10.
11.
12.

UNIT 3. Positive Interaction

Lesson 9. Witty Comments

LESSON 13

UNIT 4. CULTURAL DIVERSITY

Cultural Mistakes

Overview

- [ ] Getting Started
- [ ] Situational Dialogue
- [ ] Language Focus
- [ ] Set the Stage
- [ ] Business Basics
- [ ] Numbers and Facts

[Learning Objectives] Upon completion of this lesson, you will be able to…
- discuss the importance of cultural awareness and common cultural mistakes people make
- discuss major cultural differences between Eastern and Western cultures

1 GETTING STARTED

1 Warm up

Let's open the floor. What are your opinions?

01.
Why do you think cultural awareness is important when doing business with foreign associates? Explain.

02.
What are some examples of things you should research before engaging in a business relationship with someone from an unfamiliar culture?

03.
What are some common cultural mistakes foreigners make in your country? How would you advise them to better prepare for these situations?

2 Formal vs. Informal

Write the correct phrases in the formal or informal column of the table according to the tone.

a. That's a brilliant idea!
b. I didn't mean it like that.
c. That is such a shock!
d. Good point!
e. Wow!
f. This gesture signifies appreciation.
g. I value your input on this project.
h. I think the number 13 is unlucky.
i. That tradition makes perfect sense.
j. We do things a little differently.
k. We use that expression to signify a meeting's end.
l. My culture places a great deal of importance on punctuality.
m. Doing this with your hand means slow down.
n. Family is most important in our culture.
o. I'm sincerely sorry for the confusion.
p. It just means that you did a great job.
q. I believe pursuing happiness comes first and foremost.
s. My culture has a different view on the issue.

Function	Formal	Informal
Introducing differences		
Showing understanding		
Demonstrating cultural values		
Showing respect for others' ideas		
Talking about beliefs		
Explaining gestures		
Apologizing for misunderstanding		
Explaining idioms		
Expressing surprise		

76 Business Basics 2

2 SITUATIONAL DIALOGUE

1 Before reading the dialogue, use the information given below to answer the following questions.

James Cho
A representative from a South Korean company at an electronics trade show
MISSION
To form a closer relationship with a business associate

Mark Prichard
A representative from an American company

To make small talk with an associate while expressing needs

1. Look at the characters and describe the situation.
2. What is the relationship between the characters?
3. What do you think will happen next?

2 Practice the dialogue and answer the comprehension questions.

No Means No

James Cho: Hello, I think we met at the last conference. I'm James Cho. Mr. Prichard, right?

Mark Prichard: Nice to see you again. You can call me Mark.

James Cho: I'm going to get some coffee. Would you like some?

Mark Prichard: No, thank you.

James Cho: Are you sure?

Mark Prichard: No, that's okay. I'm fine now.

James Cho: It's no problem at all. I'm going right now.

Mark Prichard: Actually, I just had some coffee.

James Cho: Oh, I'm sorry. I asked too many times, right? In my culture, we usually offer more than once.

Mark Prichard: No problem. I didn't know about that. Maybe we could get coffee another time.

FUN FACTS

Did you know?

❶ The first US President to greet people with a handshake was Thomas Jefferson. Before that, Presidents bowed.

❷ In 2012, only 37% of US companies earned a customer experience index rating of "excellent" or "good."

Questions

1. Do you enjoy making small talk with people? What are some ways to break the ice with unfamiliar people?
2. What do you think Mr. Cho and Mr. Prichard will do next?
3. If you were Mr. Prichard, would you have accepted the coffee? Explain your reasoning.

Lesson 13. Cultural Mistakes

3 LANGUAGE FOCUS

••• KEY PATTERNS

Here are some key patterns that you can use when discussing common cultural differences and mistakes.

You can call me...
- Joe.
- by my first name.
- Sandy if you want.

I didn't know about...
- that tradition.
- the meaning of the gesture.
- the differences between our cultures.

In..., we...
- the West,…shake hands when meeting.
- my country,…avoid touching people we don't know well.
- China,…don't use that gesture.

4 SET THE STAGE

CASE SCENARIOS

Read each scenario and complete each stage.

1 Business Expressions

Read the expressions and write your own sentence using each expression.

play it by ear improvise; act instinctively rather than according to rules or a plan
Ex) There was a problem with the projector, so I just had to play it by ear when I gave my presentation.
Sentence

ring a bell sound familiar
Ex) The name rings a bell, but I can't remember where I met him.
Sentence

have a game plan to have a strategy devised before an event
Ex) This is a big meeting, so it's important that we have a game plan before going in.
Sentence

Scenario #1
Role A: **Customer Service Representative**
Role B: **New Client**

You are working at a wholesale chemical company and meeting with a new American customer for the first time. The client is older, but insists that you address him by his first name. He asks you questions about your life and interests. Introduce yourself and make small talk in order to establish a personal relationship before conducting business.

Stage 1. Brainstorm the mission of each character.

Stage 2. Role play.
Be sure to complete the mission of each character and use at least 2 key patterns.

Scenario #2
Role A: **Employee transferred from an overseas branch**
Role B: **Local employee**

You are helping to orient an Albanian employee to your company. The new employee has many questions about office procedures as well as Korean culture. Provide answers to his questions and compare his and your culture.

Stage 1. Brainstorm the mission of each character.

Stage 2. Role play.
Be sure to complete the mission of each character and use at least 2 key patterns.

5 BUSINESS BASICS

Cultural Mistakes

An "onion model" is one way to represent and understand culture. Just as an onion has many layers, so does the culture of any group. Also, just like an onion, there is a core to each culture. The outer layers are the expressions, ritual, actions, and behaviors which are readily apparent. The inner core, or the foundation, of the culture is the value system, which influences the other aspects. Having some culture shock strategies can keep you from feeling overwhelmed when the culture shock does finally occur. Culture shock happens to everyone in varying degrees. The key difference is how you cope with it. Take a look below.

Preventing Culture Shock	
Tip	**Reason/Attribute**
Find an Expat	Find someone from your country who has already "made" it in country and can show you the ropes.
Write in a Journal	Writing is considered therapeutic since your thoughts can be manifested.
See the Beauty	Visit places of high culture and attend cultural entertainment. Seeing value in the culture will create respect and interest.
Establish a Routine	Routine equals stability, especially if it focuses on building core traits: e.g., mental and physical health, career/academic success, or proper social outlets.
Humor/Levity	Being able to "laugh at yourself" and deal with imperfection is a characteristic that you will need everywhere.
Get to Immigrants	Meeting, understanding, and assisting immigrants in your own country can give you insight, sympathy, and perspective when heading abroad yourself. You could come across some good luck, too.

Share Your Thoughts

1. Which of the above tips do you think would be most handy when traveling abroad? Have you tried any yourself? What was the result?

2. When travelling abroad, some people struggle to adapt to the food of the other country. Do you have any advice or experience in this regard?

3. Some cultures, particularly Arabic Muslim cultures, are notable for giving thanks to and referencing their religion in many contexts, even business. Do you think that different ethnicities and religions should be more discreet about their religion, or is it better to be outspoken?

Lesson 13. Cultural Mistakes

6 NUMBERS & FACTS

Cultural Note

The Azeri culture of **Azerbaijan** is very superstitious, so be aware of different acts to court good luck and ward off bad luck. For example, when someone leaves on a long business trip, Azeris will toss a bowl of water behind that person as a way of bringing good luck and a safe journey.

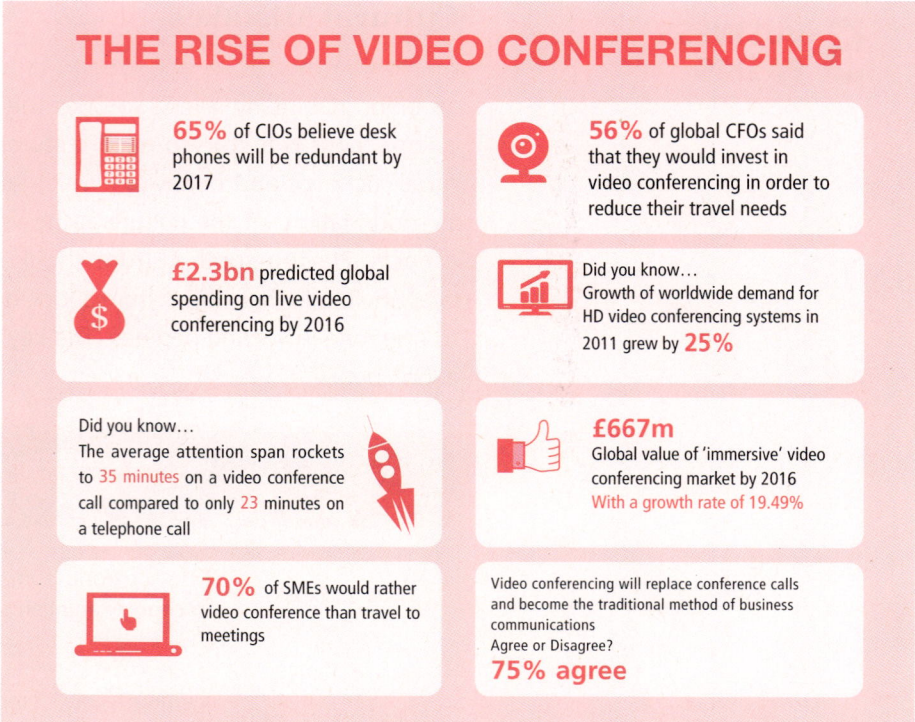

THE RISE OF VIDEO CONFERENCING

- **65%** of CIOs believe desk phones will be redundant by 2017
- **56%** of global CFOs said that they would invest in video conferencing in order to reduce their travel needs
- **£2.3bn** predicted global spending on live video conferencing by 2016
- Did you know… Growth of worldwide demand for HD video conferencing systems in 2011 grew by **25%**
- Did you know… The average attention span rockets to 35 minutes on a video conference call compared to only 23 minutes on a telephone call
- **£667m** Global value of 'immersive' video conferencing market by 2016 With a growth rate of 19.49%
- **70%** of SMEs would rather video conference than travel to meetings
- Video conferencing will replace conference calls and become the traditional method of business communications Agree or Disagree? **75% agree**

Look at the image above to answer the following questions.

1. What percentage of people believe that video conferencing will eventually replace conference calls in business communication?
2. Why do you believe 56% of CFOs said they would invest in video conferencing in order to reduce travel? Why might this be more cost effective?
3. Use the data to explain the growth potential of conference calls. Are they common in your workplace?

Share 3 new things you learned from this lesson:

1. _____

2. _____

3. _____

7 REVIEW & PREVIEW

 **Sneak Peek**

1. If departing for a business trip abroad, how much do you focus on cultural etiquette as part of the success of the trip?
2. By practicing another culture's etiquette, do you ever feel like you are violating your own principles? Do you find it hard to act in a way that is not according to your own culture?

LESSON 14

UNIT 4. CULTURAL DIVERSITY

Cross-cultural Business Etiquette

Overview

- [ ] Getting Started
- [ ] Situational Dialogue
- [ ] Language Focus
- [ ] Set the Stage
- [ ] Business Basics
- [ ] Numbers and Facts

[Learning Objectives]   Upon completion of this lesson, you will be able to…
- recognize different cross-cultural values
- explore global business manner, etiquette, and protocol

1 GETTING STARTED

1 Warm up

Let's open the floor. What are your opinions?

01.
What are some factors that affect business etiquette in your country? Explain.

02.
How would you prepare to do business with someone from an unfamiliar culture? What questions would you ask?

03.
What kind of things do you think are most important in your country's business culture? Are they things that you personally feel important?

2 Formal vs. Informal

Write the correct phrases in the formal or informal column of the table according to the tone.

a. I'm sorry, but that doesn't sound right.
b. I didn't get what you said.
c. Excuse me.
d. I believe that is incorrect.
e. I don't think that is right.
f. Don't forget to bring a present.
g. Could I please add something?
h. You can benefit from my experience.
i. Remember to be punctual for all meetings.
j. You raise a good point, but I have to disagree.
k. You should not cross your legs when we meet with the Saudi Arabians.
l. Maybe she said no because she doesn't eat pork.
m. When entering a business function, the most senior person present should always be given special treatment.
n. Could you please repeat that number one more time?
o. He might be late because punctuality is not as important in Argentinean culture.
p. The meeting will be a working breakfast, so be prepared to wake up early.
q. I lived there for 4 years, so I can give you a few pointers.
r. It's rude to say no when the host offers you a drink.

Function	Formal	Informal
Asking to repeat information		
Commenting on an error		
Interrupting		
Offering an explanation		
Discussing etiquette		
Politely disagreeing		
Offering tips		
Demonstrating expertise		
Discussing protocol		

Lesson 14. Cross-cultural Business Etiquette

2 SITUATIONAL DIALOGUE

1 Before reading the dialogue, use the information given below to answer the following questions.

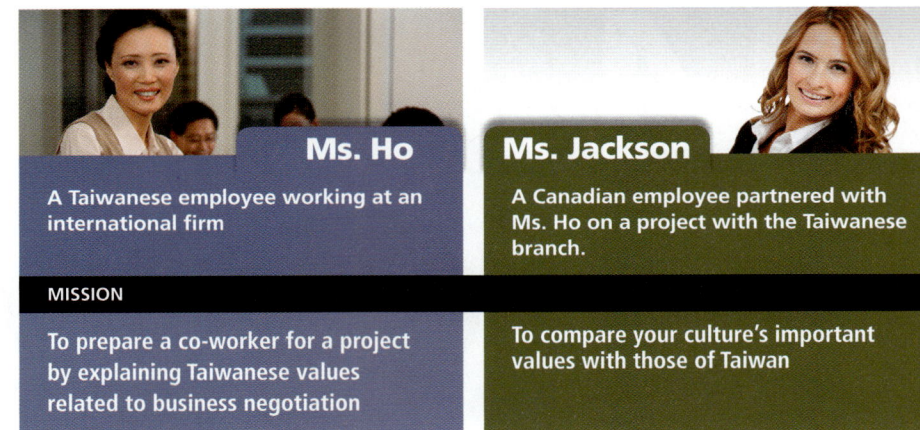

Ms. Ho
A Taiwanese employee working at an international firm

MISSION
To prepare a co-worker for a project by explaining Taiwanese values related to business negotiation

Ms. Jackson
A Canadian employee partnered with Ms. Ho on a project with the Taiwanese branch.

To compare your culture's important values with those of Taiwan

1. Look at the characters and describe the situation
2. What is the relationship between the characters?
3. What do you think will happen next?

2 Practice the dialogue and answer the comprehension questions.

What's Most Important To You?

Ms. Ho: I consider relationships as the most important part of the negotiation process in Taiwan.

Ms. Jackson: I'm sorry. I didn't catch what you said. It's a little loud in here.

Ms. Ho: Relationships...it's critical that we establish relationships with our partners as soon as possible in order to carry out a successful negotiation.

Ms. Jackson: I guess that's pretty similar to the West. How can we accomplish that in Taiwan?

Ms. Ho: In the beginning, we need to prepare gifts for our partners and be sure to always show respect for everyone in the room.

Ms. Jackson: Is there anything else I should be careful about?

Ms. Ho: Giving business cards with one hand is considered rude.

Ms. Jackson: How should I hand out my card?

Ms. Ho: You should present it with two hands and make sure to pay respect to another person's card.

Ms. Jackson: I'll take that into account.

Questions

1. Do you feel the values described in the dialogue are similar to your country's? Why or why not?
2. What is most important to you in life? Justify your response.
3. What steps do you take to establish relationships with new business partners? Explain.

82 Business Basics 2

3 LANGUAGE FOCUS

••• KEY PATTERNS

Here are some key patterns that you can use when discussing differing cultural values and etiquette.

I consider... to be the most important...
- personal relations… part of the sales process.
- my employees… tool at my disposal.
- the clients…factor.

... is consider rude.
- Blowing your nose at the table
- Eating with your mouth open
- Answering your phone during a meeting

I'm sorry; I didn't catch...
- your name.
- what you said.
- what your position is.

4 SET THE STAGE

CASE SCENARIOS

Read each scenario and complete each stage.

1 Business Expressions

Read the expressions and write your own sentence using each expression.

fall through the cracks to get lost or be forgotten
Ex) I think that part of the report fell through the cracks.
Sentence

cut to the chase to skip of the unimportant details and deal with the main point
Ex) Let me cut to the chase. Your behavior in the meeting was unacceptable.
Sentence

stay on your toes to stay aware and energetic
Ex) There's only a few hours left before the big presentation, so you are really going to have to stay on your toes.
Sentence

Scenario #1

 Role A: **Employee 1 (preparing for a conference)**
 Role B: **Employee 2 (has experience working at a similar conference)**

You are an employee at a software company preparing to meet with international customers at a sales conference for new products. Discuss how to prepare for the diverse cultural backgrounds of the clients with an experienced co-worker. Discuss international business card culture with your co-worker.

Stage 1. Brainstorm the mission of each character.

Stage 2. Role play.
Be sure to complete the mission of each character and use at least 2 key patterns.

Scenario #2

 Role A: **Co-worker 1**
 Role B: **Co-worker 2**

You are having lunch with a co-worker who just returned from a long business trip abroad. Discuss your co-worker's experiences. Ask questions about how people address each other in business environments and compare them to your own culture. Try to consider the reasons behind the cultural norms.

Stage 1. Brainstorm the mission of each character.

Stage 2. Role play.
Be sure to complete the mission of each character and use at least 2 key patterns.

5 SITUATIONAL DIALOGUE

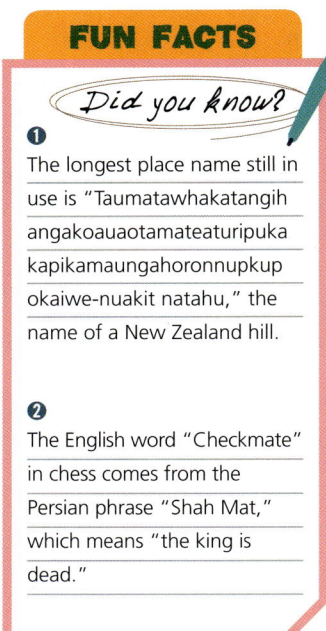

FUN FACTS

Did you know?

❶ The longest place name still in use is "Taumatawhakatangihangakoauaotamateaturipukakapikamaungahoronnupkupokaiwe-nuakit natahu," the name of a New Zealand hill.

❷ The English word "Checkmate" in chess comes from the Persian phrase "Shah Mat," which means "the king is dead."

Cultural Mistakes

One of the ways to analyze culture is according to something called the Power Distance Index (PDI), devised by the social psychologist Geert Hofstede. This index indicates to what degree each culture expects and accepts that power and decision-making will be unequally shared. Being mindful of each culture's PDI could let you know how your business partners in that country will make decisions.

According to country, certain manners will distinguish you as sensitive and worth doing business with. Breaking some of the cultural codes and business etiquette points may make you an outsider. How well-versed are you in other countries' fine points of etiquette?

Etiquette Points

Country	Tip
Japan	Receive a business card with two hands; study it carefully and show respect to it.
Middle East	Avoid giving or presenting objects made from pig skin. Pigs are considered unclean.
Russia	Show patience in the face of double standards. Prime example: You must be on time even if your Russian counterpart is very late.
Middle East	Eyes somewhat closed indicates a state of deep thinking, not sleepiness or disregard.
Brazil	Brazilians stand very close and use physical contact. Being close shows trust.
India	Due to notions of politeness, "yes" might actually mean "no", so be sure to check the depth and commitment for a true "yes."

Share Your Thoughts

1. Complete the table with one more tip for another country.
   Which foreign business etiquette would you find most confusing or frustrating to deal with?

2. Would you ever reject a business deal with a foreigner just because he or she violated your country's etiquette, or do you concentrate primarily on the financial, business aspects of the deal?

3. If you ever make a cultural etiquette mistake in a foreign country, how could you better your image?

6 NUMBERS & FACTS

Cultural Note

In Russia, never shake hands or hand things over a threshold. It is considered unlucky. So, if you order pizza delivery, you must walk out to the deliverer or invite the person inside across the threshold.

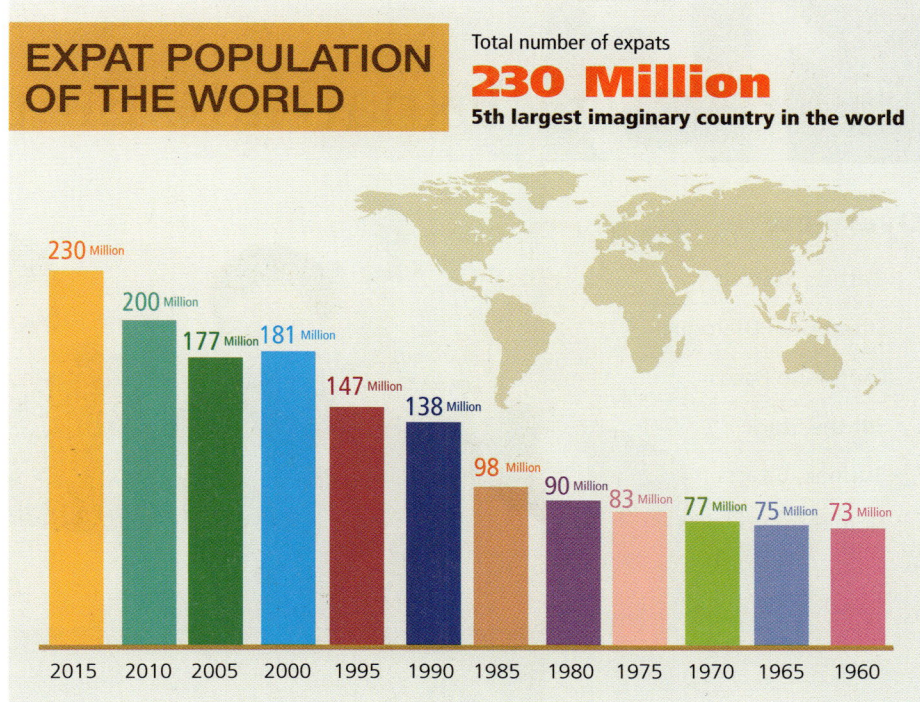

Look at the image above to answer the following questions.

1. How many expats were living abroad in 1995.?

2. Use the chart to describe how the number of expats has grown since 1960.? Which 5 year period had the largest increase? How could this be explained?

3. What might have caused the growth in the number of expats over the past century? Do you feel this data reflects change in your country?

Share 3 new things you learned from this lesson:

1.

2.

3.

7 REVIEW & PREVIEW

 **Sneak Peek**

1. If your company unexpectedly required you to move abroad for 1-2 years to a country which does not appeal to you, how would you react?
What criteria would you use to decide whether you accept or reject the request?

2. What could be the best effect of working abroad for many years?
What is the worst effect that could happen as a result?

LESSON 15

UNIT 4. CULTURAL DIVERSITY

Expatriate Employees

Overview

- [ ] Getting Started
- [ ] Situational Dialogue
- [ ] Language Focus
- [ ] Set the Stage
- [ ] Business Basics
- [ ] Numbers and Facts

[Learning Objectives] Upon completion of this lesson, you will be able to…
- recognize cultural challenges expatriates face abroad
- discuss ways to ease the transition into a new culture

1 GETTING STARTED

1 Warm up

Let's open the floor. What are your opinions?

01.
What questions would you ask before leaving for a new country for work? Explain.

02.
Have you ever worked or studied abroad? What challenges did you encounter?

03.
What advice would you give a foreigner preparing to move to your country for work? Explain.

2 Formal vs. Informal

Write the correct phrases in the formal or informal column of the table according to the tone.

a. When are you going?
b. What if I don't like it?
c. Try reading a guidebook.
d. Need a pointer?
e. Thanks for the tip.
f. What did you agree to?
g. Thank you for your kind advice.
h. Could I give you a little advice?
i. Did you hear the good news?
j. Additionally, you should avoid calling superiors by their first name.
k. Could you tell me what to expect in the negotiation?
l. It was just announced that our office will be relocated to Bangkok.
m. How long will you be working there?
n. Have you considered taking a language class?
o. I'm just worried about culture shock.
p. Tell me more about the office culture.
q. Also, we need to submit the plan by Tuesday.
r. When will you be departing?

Function	Formal	Informal
Offering advice		
Asking about a schedule		
Asking about a commitment		
Bringing up a concern		
Making a suggestion		
Requesting information		
Sharing new information		
Adding information		
Expressing gratitude		

2 SITUATIONAL DIALOGUE

1 Before reading the dialogue, use the information given below to answer the following questions.

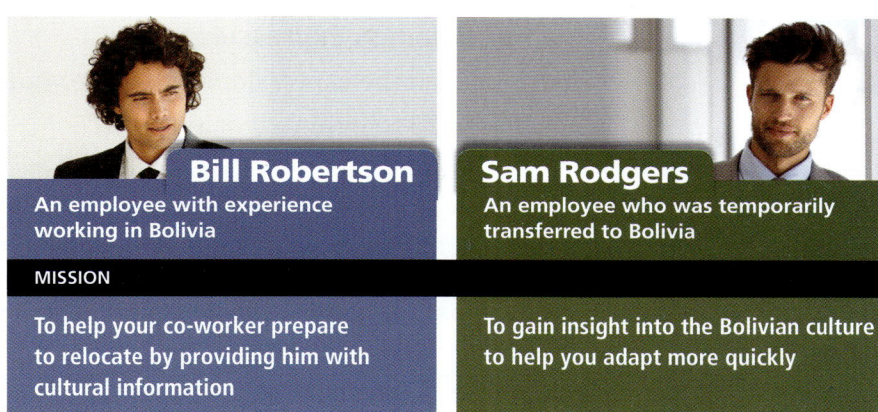

Bill Robertson
An employee with experience working in Bolivia

Sam Rodgers
An employee who was temporarily transferred to Bolivia

MISSION

To help your co-worker prepare to relocate by providing him with cultural information

To gain insight into the Bolivian culture to help you adapt more quickly

1. Look at the characters and describe the situation.
2. What is the relationship between the characters?
3. What do you think will happen next?

2 Practice the dialogue and answer the comprehension questions.

Advice from a Former Expat

Bill Robertson: Hey, Sam. What's up? When do you leave for Bolivia?

Sam Rodgers: Next Saturday. I have to tell you that I'm getting a little nervous now. I found out about the transfer so suddenly that I haven't had time to research.

Bill Robertson: Don't worry. I'm sure you'll like it there. For me, the most challenging thing about living there was being away from my family, but you'll be okay. Your wife is going, too, right?

Sam Rodgers: I guess you're right. It could be worse. Is there anything that you wish you knew before you left?

Bill Robertson: I suggest you bring some good books if you read a lot. English books are really expensive there.

Sam Rodgers: That's good advice. How was the working environment there?

Bill Robertson: It's fairly relaxed. I think you'll enjoy it there.

Sam Rodgers: Thanks for that. You've really reassured me.

Bill Robertson: No problem. I've got to get back to work.

Sam Rodgers: Okay. See you around.

Questions

1. If you had to prepare for an international move, what products would you absolutely need to bring along? Are there any brands or items from your country that you couldn't imagine living without? Explain.
2. If you had the opportunity to work in any country, where would you go? Why?
3. If you were Sam Rodgers, what other questions would you ask?

Lesson 15. Expatriate Employees

3 LANGUAGE FOCUS

••• KEY PATTERNS

Here are some key patterns that you can use when discussing adapting to cultural differences when living abroad.

I suggest that…
- you observe what other people do and copy them.
- you buy a good dictionary.
- you read this book about expat life.

The most challenging thing about… was…
- working abroad…being away from my family.
- adjusting…the time difference.
- moving here…getting used to the food.

I have to tell you that…
- it will get easier.
- you will adjust soon.
- my overall experience was good.

4 SET THE STAGE

CASE SCENARIOS

Read each scenario and complete each stage.

1 Business Expressions

Read the expressions and write your own sentence using each expression.

break even to reach a point when profits equal costs
Ex) I think with the new clients this quarter we will be able to break even.
Sentence _____

loss for words to be speechless; in shock
Ex) When I heard the deal fell through, I was at a loss for words.
Sentence _____

blow a deal to cause a deal to fall through
Ex) His careless mistake was what blew the deal.
Sentence _____

Scenario #1 Role A: **Co-worker 1** (Preparing to take a position at an overseas branch)
Role B: **Co-worker 2** (Has experience working abroad)

You have just been assigned a position to work in your country's Indonesian branch. You have some concerns about the culture of the office and difficulties that you might face as an expat. Ask questions to find out what to expect as you transition to life in Jakarta.

Stage 1. Brainstorm the mission of each character.
_____

Stage 2. Role play.
  Be sure to complete the mission of each character and use at least 2 key patterns.

Scenario #2 Role A: **Employee**   Role B: **Spouse**

You have just been assigned a project that requires you to collaborate with one of your company's Singapore offices. For the project, you will need to relocate to Singapore for at least six months. Inform your family of the news and answer questions that they might have.

Stage 1. Brainstorm the mission of each character.
_____

Stage 2. Role play.
  Be sure to complete the mission of each character and use at least 2 key patterns.

5 BUSINESS BASICS

Business Basics

As businesses become increasingly globalized, companies need to place more workers abroad. Even with more powerful communication technology, it is necessary to have some "feet on the ground" to connect with the locals. Really, there is no substitute for face-to-face encounters and bridge building. "Expat" in business terms means someone who lives abroad, away from their native country, for an extended length of time. Many businesses in the global market opt to hire expat employees and diversify their HR pool. This diversity in the workforce has both advantages and disadvantages. Look at the table below.

The two columns below are independent of each other. Each one represents some of the benefits and challenges of a diverse workforce.	
Benefits	**Challenges**
Chance to learn about different cultures	Working on the same project means longer time required for communication
Source of new ideas outside the restrictions and frames of local culture	Different understanding of the same idea
Get a new set of eyes to analyze your company: strengths/weaknesses; public image; ways to innovate	Dealing with different cultural behaviors: personal space, touching, gestures, manners, forms of politeness
Insights into marketing and targeting your product to a foreign audience	Might encounter views that you consider deeply antithetical to your own such as views on women, history, etc.
More focus on how the company culture unites people of various backgrounds	Burden to help the employee outside of the office as well to adjust to life overall, resulting in more responsibilities
Experience on building relationship, a handy skill especially useful when traveling abroad	The foreigner may have made a mistake in coming abroad or lacks commitment

Share Your Thoughts

1. Brainstorm and add more benefits and challenges to working with a diverse workforce. Which outweighs the other?

2. If you had to live for a year or more abroad, how might your life change? Would your personality change in any way?

3. Should companies be more considerate about assigning a worker abroad who is married and has children, or do you think marital and family status is minor compared to someone's salary size, talent, and position within the company?

FUN FACTS

Did you know?

❶ Immigrants make up 12.5% of small business owners in the USA.

❷ In 2010, according to UN statics, more than 200 million people were working outside of their home country.

Lesson 15. Expatriate Employees

6 NUMBERS & FACTS

Cultural Note

Moroccans show much affection during a greeting. In fact, a handshake could last up to ten minutes. Also, a typical gesture is to touch the heart after shaking hands as a way to show the warmth and value of the encounter.

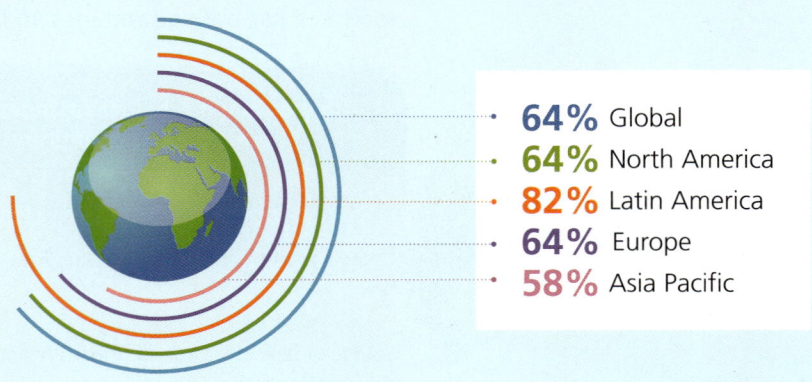

ADJUSTMENT PROBLEMS LEAD TO ASSIGNMENT FAILURE

Nearly 2/3 of multinational companies responding to Mercer's 2012 Worldwide Survey of International Assignment Policies and Practices cite assignees' difficulty in adjusting to the host location as a primary reason for assignment failure.

Percentage of employers who say difficulty adjusting to the host country is a key factor in assignment failure.

- **64%** Global
- **64%** North America
- **82%** Latin America
- **64%** Europe
- **58%** Asia Pacific

Look at the image above to answer the following questions.

1. What percentage of North American employers said that difficulties adjusting to the host country were a key factor in assignment failure?

2. Which region claimed the highest percentage of adjustment problems? The lowest? What inferences could you make about the difference?

3. What are some factors that could lead to adjustment difficulties? How could an expat prepare for them?

Share 3 new things you learned from this lesson:

1.

2.

3.

7 REVIEW & PREVIEW

 Sneak Peek

1. A foreign friend is coming to visit you, and he would like to know what is considered polite or rude in your country. What advice would you give him?

2. Do you think foreigners, such as temporary visitors, should be exempt from the standards of cultural enforcement regarding rude gestures?

LESSON 16

UNIT 4. CULTURAL DIVERSITY

Body Language Across Cultures

Overview

- [ ] Getting Started
- [ ] Situational Dialogue
- [ ] Language Focus
- [ ] Set the Stage
- [ ] Business Basics
- [ ] Numbers and Facts

[Learning Objectives] Upon completion of this lesson, you will be able to…
- review gestures and nonverbal communication of other countries
- understand the concept of personal space in different cultures and discuss how it is incorporated in business

1 GETTING STARTED

1 Warm up

Let's open the floor. What are your opinions?

01.
What differences have you observed between your country's body language and that of other countries?

02.
How would you explain your culture's beliefs about personal space to a foreign visitor?

03.
Why is it important to be aware of body language and other norms of non-verbal communication when interacting with people from other cultures?

2 Formal vs. Informal

Write the correct phrases in the formal or informal column of the table according to the tone.

a. I'm sorry that I misunderstood.
b. What is the significance of doing that?
c. I observed that people talk more animatedly.
d. No worries.
e. I'm sorry, but do you mind if I change chairs?
f. No problem. I completely understand.
g. Don't forget to bring a present.
h. Completely my misunderstanding.
i. Is it okay if I open a window?
j. That gesture means something very different in Italy.
k. Why did you make that gesture?
l. In my country, we tend to value personal space more.
m. In contrast to the US, initial meetings can often seem very formal.
n. It seems to me that punctuality is not as important.
o. In Greece, it's normal for several people to speak at the same time.
p. A clenched fist is a sign of defiance or solidarity.
q. To demonstrate that something is unsatisfactory put your thumb down.
r. You should avoid exchanging business cards at social occasions.

Function	Formal	Informal
Accepting an apology		
Apologizing for misunderstanding		
Discussing cultural norms		
Commenting on differences		
Expressing discomfort		
Offering advice		
Making an observation		
Describing a gesture		
Asking for an explanation		

Lesson 16. Body Language Across Cultures

2 SITUATIONAL DIALOGUE

1 Before reading the dialogue, use the information given below to answer the following questions.

Mr. Lawson
An American employee who has been working in the Istanbul branch of an international company for 3 years

MISSION
To help a newcomer adjust to a foreign culture

Mr. Jasper
An American employee who was transferred to the Istanbul branch 2 weeks ago

To improve his communication skills by learning about the cultural norms of the country that he is working in

1. Look at the characters and describe the situation
2. What is the relationship between the characters?
3. What do you think will happen next?

2 Practice the dialogue and answer the comprehension questions.

An Offensive Gesture

Mr. Lawson: Good morning, Mr. Jasper. How are you doing today?

Mr. Jasper: (Mouth is full, so he makes an O.K. sign.)

Mr. Lawson: You're new to Turkey, so you might not know this. I don't think it's such a great idea to use that gesture around the office. It's considered offensive here.

Mr. Jasper: I'm sorry. I didn't intend to offend anyone.

Mr. Lawson: I know you didn't. That's why I'm telling you now.

Mr. Jasper: Thanks for letting me know. Are there any other gestures that I should be aware of?

Mr. Lawson: There are a few others, but most aren't things you would do by accident. For example, you should avoid making a fist with your thumb between your index finger and middle finger.

Mr. Jasper: Good to know. I'm worried about how many people I might have accidentally offended now.

Mr. Lawson: Don't worry. People will understand, because you're still learning the culture.

Mr. Jasper: I guess you're right.

Questions

1. What does the "okay" sign mean in your culture? Do you use it often? Explain.
2. Are there any gestures in your country that are offensive? How would you explain them to a foreigner?
3. How could you apologize if you offended someone else? Why is it important to do so?

3 LANGUAGE FOCUS

••• KEY PATTERNS

Here are some key patterns that you can use when explaining cultural differences in body language.

I didn't intend to...
- offend you.
- cause confusion.
- upset our guests.

I don't think it's such a great idea to...
- include that image in the report.
- cross your arms during the presentation.
- use that gesture in front of the visitors.

You should avoid ...ing
- shaking hands with them.
- handing things with your left hand.
- calling them by their first names.

1 Business Expressions

Read the expressions and write your own sentence using each expression.

bring to the table **what one can offer or provide**
Ex) I'm happy to have Kevin join our team. He really has a lot to bring to the table.
Sentence

earth-shattering news **news of enormous importance or consequence**
Ex) Hearing that our partners were pulling out of the project was earth-shattering news.
Sentence

draw the line **reasonably object to something or set a limit**
Ex) We really need to draw the line about personal phone calls during working hours.
Sentence

4 SET THE STAGE

CASE SCENARIOS

Read each scenario and complete each stage.

Scenario #1

Role A: **Asian employee**   Role B: **Western employee**

You are working on a team with several foreign employees. During a team meeting, you sat a little closer than what one member felt was appropriate. Later, the employee tells you about how uncomfortable he or she was by explaining his or her culture's idea of personal space. Listen to the explanation and apologize.

Stage 1. Brainstorm the mission of each character.

Stage 2. Role play.
Be sure to complete the mission of each character and use at least 2 key patterns.

Scenario #2

Role A: **Supervisor**   Role B: **Foreign Employee**

You need to talk to a foreign employee of your branch about their use of body language and gestures. Other employees are understanding of the cultural differences, but some of the gestures could be considered offensive. Talk about how gestures mean different things in different cultures. For example, the "okay" sign means zero in France, "okay" in English-speaking countries and money to the Japanese. Advise the employee about gestures to avoid in your country.

Stage 1. Brainstorm the mission of each character.

Stage 2. Role play.
Be sure to complete the mission of each character and use at least 2 key patterns.

5 BUSINESS BASICS

FUN FACTS

Did you know?

❶ In 1977, Ken Olsen, the president of DEC Computers, said, "There is no reason why anyone would want a computer in their home."

❷ 87% of global consumers believe business should place at least equal emphasis on social interests as business interests, and "purpose" has increased as a purchase trigger by 26% since 2008.

Cultures and Body Language

As much as the words we use and our tone of voice, our body also imparts communicative information. Our stance, posture, and gestures all signal some information either purposefully or unconsciously. Facial expressions, movements of hands and feet, position of the body, and even the order of movements convey meaning. Whereas some of these attributes are instinctive human behavior, many have been molded and refined according to culture.

The table below lists some common gestures found around the world and localized in a particular culture. Have you encountered any of these before? What was the consequence? Do you consider yourself culturally fluent for international business? Take a look.

Gestures

Gesture	Description	Meaning	
Thumbs-up	The thumb is raised vertically and the rest of the fingers are clenched in a fist.	US	Approval
		Greece	Insult
Okay sign	With hand turned outward, the thumb and forefinger make a circle. The other three fingers spread out.	US	Okay
		Japan	Money
		France	Zero
V-sign (palm outward)	Also known as the peace sign. The forefinger and middle finger point up in a V	Brazil	Horrible offense
		US	Peace sign or
		Britain	Symbol of victory in
The "Corna"	Resembles a set of horns. With the palm facing outward, the index and little fingers extend up while the rest clench together.	U.S.	Rock 'n roll music gesture; sports gesture for University of Texas Longhorns;
		Buddhist and Hindu	Known as the "Karana Mudra," it is used to dispel evil
The "Fig"	Clenching the fingers together in fist and sticking out the thumb between the index and middle finger.	European cultures	IInsult (your wife is cheating; sexual insult)

Share Your Thoughts

1. What other gestures do you think that the class should know? Fill in the table above and share with the class.

2. How do you feel about gestures in general? Do you think that gestures are silly or do you see them as powerful, cultural symbols and signs?

3. Sometimes high level diplomats and officials make mistakes with their body language. For example, some Koreans found it offensive when Bill Gates kept his left hand in his pants pocket when greeting South Korean president Park Geun-hye. How much should such gestural errors influence business?

6 NUMBERS & FACTS

Cultural Note

To signal appreciation or to impart a positive feeling, *a Brazilian* might pinch his or her earlobe with the thumb and forefinger. To add dramatic emphasis to this gesture, some Brazilians might even reach behind their head and pinch the opposite earlobe.

7 REVIEW & PREVIEW

COMMON NONVERBAL MISTAKES MADE AT A JOB INTERVIEW

- **47%** Having little or no knowledge of the company is the most common mistake job seekers make during interviews
- **21%** Playing with hair or touching face
- **67%** Failure to make eye contact
- **38%** Lack of smile
- **33%** Bad posture
- **21%** Crossing arms over their chest
- **9%** Using too many hand gestures
- **26%** Handshake that is too weak
- **33%** Fidgeting too much

In a survey of 2000 bosses, 33% claimed that they know within 90 seconds of an interview whether they will hire someone

The average length of an interview is approximately 40 minutes

When meeting new people, the first impression is made by:
- **7%** What we say
- **38%** The quality of our voice, grammar and overall confidence
- **55%** The way we dress, act and walk through the door

Clothes
- **70%** Employers claim they don't want applicants to be fashionable or trendy
- **65%** Of bosses said clothes could be the deciding factor between two similar candidates

Look at the image above to answer the following questions.

1. What percentage of bosses surveyed considered a weak handshake a common nonverbal mistake?

2. Present the statistics about factors that make an impact when meeting new people. Why do you think nonverbal factors have such a strong effect?

3. Read through the "Common nonverbal mistakes made at a job interview." Are you guilty of any of these behaviors? Which ones bother you?

Share 3 new things you learned from this lesson:

1.

2.

3.

 Let's look back

1. Imagine that your company put you in charge of training young workers on going abroad for the first time for business trips. How would you train the young workers to be adept at international business? Would you design a program or training manual?

2. Key phrases, slogans, and/or mottos can be an apt and concise way to summarize a rule or way to act. Being mindful of such advice can increase your success. Please use your personal knowledge and lessons from this book to make a guideline for international business.

CASE STUDY
Globalization and Business Cultural Awareness

Background

Globalization means that more people are doing business abroad today than ever before. As a result, there is a need to be prepared to assimilate to unfamiliar cultures. Many people feel that it is important to learn all that they can about the country they will be working in before beginning a new job assignment.

By doing this, they can show respect for their business partners and avoid accidentally offending others. At the same time, others think it is unfair that they are obligated to spend time learning cultural rules for short business commitments. They argue that people engaging in business with foreigners should be more understanding of mistakes.

UNIT 4.
Cultural Diversity

Tasks

01
Finish the card with reasons for learning about other cultures' etiquette (pro.) and reasons against it (con.) Add some of your own ideas to the chart.

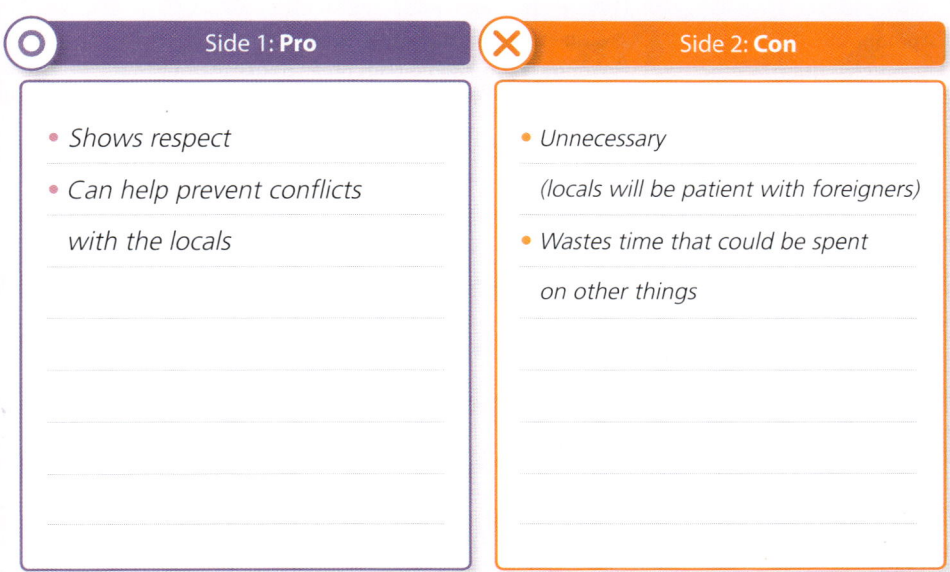

Side 1: Pro	Side 2: Con
• Shows respect • Can help prevent conflicts with the locals	• Unnecessary (locals will be patient with foreigners) • Wastes time that could be spent on other things

02
Compare your points with a partner. Did you write down the same things? Choose sides and debate.

03
Image you are helping a foreign friend prepare to work in your country. What aspects of your country's culture do you feel that your friend most needs to be aware of? Write down what you feel are the top three points and present your list to the class.

1.

2.

3.

Answer Key — Getting Started – Formal vs. Informal

Unit 1. Professional Communicator

Lesson 1 – Telephoning & Note-Taking

Function	Formal	Informal
Greeting	How do you do?	Hi there.
Asking after health	How are you?	How is it going?
Offering	May I offer any of you another drink?	Drink, anyone?
Asking for someone	Could you put me through to Ms. Jones, please?	Is Monica there?
Asking for repetition	Would you mind repeating that for me?	Excuse me?
Apologizing	I do beg your pardon.	Sorry.
Asking for directions	I wonder if you could direct me to the restroom?	Where are the toilets?
Making arrangements	I will telephone you after six o'clock.	I'll call you later.
Saying good-bye	It has been a pleasure to meet you.	Bye.

Lesson 2 – Communication & Culture

Function	Formal	Informal
Asking for clarification	I'm sorry, but could you explain that again?	What do you mean?
Apologizing	I'd like to apologize for my mistake.	Sorry.
Offering a compliment	You did excellent work on the last project.	Great work!
Accepting a compliment	Thank you for your kind words.	Thanks.
Introducing others	Ms. Adams, I'd like to introduce you to Mr. Gregg.	Ms. Jones, Mr. Smith.
Refusing a drink	No, thank you. I'm fine.	I'm okay.
Excusing yourself from a conversation	Please excuse me for a minute.	I'll be back in a minute.
Expressing understanding	I understand your point.	I got it.
Asking for an opinion	I would like to hear your thoughts on the issue.	What do you think?

Lesson 3 – Presentation Know-how

Function	Formal	Informal
Greeting an audience	Good morning, ladies and gentlemen.	Hi, everyone.
Encouraging questions	Does anyone have anything to ask?	Any questions?
Introducing another speaker	I would like to turn the floor over to Mr. James.	Joe has a few things he wants to say now.
Addressing a specific audience member	Do you have something to add, Mr. Dale?	Yes, Ms. Marks?
Introducing a topic	We will begin by discussing new business.	Let's start now.
Closing a presentation	And with that, I will conclude my presentation.	I think we're done here.
Drawing attention to an image	Could everyone please refer to diagram 3?	Check out this chart.
Explaining a graph	As you can see in the graph, sales have increased steadily over the past year.	This graph shows a good improvement.
Presenting statistics	Our research shows a 2% increase in sales of the product.	Sales have gone up 10% in the last few weeks.

Lesson 4 – Situational Communication Strategies

Function	Formal	Informal
Expressing sympathy	I was very upset to hear about your situation.	I'm so sorry to hear about your problem.
Commenting on mood	You seem to be upset about something.	You look tired today.
Asking about a problem	What seems to be the problem?	What's wrong?
Complimenting one's work	Your job performance has been excellent lately.	Nice work!
Expressing concern	I was concerned that something was wrong.	I'm worried about you.
Offering help	Could you use some assistance?	Need some help?
Asking for help	Would you mind assisting me?	Little help, please?
Asking someone to talk	Could I speak with you for a minute?	Got some time?
Offering a solution	I believe I have an answer to your problem.	I've got an idea!

BUSINESS BASICS 2

Unit 2. Winning Negotiator

Lesson 5 – Proposal & Negotiation

Function	Formal	Informal
Introducing an idea	I have an opportunity to discuss with you.	I've got something for you.
Inviting interest	You might be interested in this investment.	You'll be interested in this.
Recommending something	I would recommend diversifying your portfolio.	You should try this stock.
Addressing doubt	I understand your concern, but you don't need to worry.	Don't worry. It's not too good to be true.
Hinting at a request	Have you considered trying our newer model?	What do you think about extending your contract?
Asking for more time	Could I please have a day or two to think about it?	Let me think it over.
Asking for more information	Could you please give me some more information about the product?	What else?
Refusing	I'm sorry, but I can't agree to that.	No, thanks.
Agreeing	I can accept your terms.	That sounds great!

Lesson 6 – Tackling Problems

Function	Formal	Informal
Bringing up a mistake	I just became aware of an error in our report.	There's something wrong with the data.
Suggesting a compromise	I could offer you a discount if you purchase more units.	I can meet you halfway on this.
Offering gentle criticism	In the future, you should be more careful.	Next time, double check your facts.
Considering risks	If the negotiation fails, we will lose a great deal of money.	If things don't work out, we will go out of business.
Agreeing to disagree	We are both entitled to an opinion.	You can think that if you want.
Finding common ground	This deal will benefit both of us.	We can both say yes to this.
Offering a solution	It might be helpful to change our approach.	We should try calling him directly.
Settling on a course of action	We should research more and reevaluate the situation.	Let's try that.
Evaluating a solution	It seems to be working.	Looks good so far.

Lesson 7 – International Negotiations

Function	Formal	Informal
Noting a difference	There seems to be a cultural difference.	We don't do that in our country.
Offering a condition	We can accept your offer if you meet this demand.	We can settle for a 5% discount.
Asking to seek approval	I'll need to get approval from the head office.	We'll need to check with the board.
Making a counteroffer	Would you consider accepting a little less?	What do you think about settling for $20 a meter?
Asking to confirm	Could you please confirm some of those details?	Is this right?
Disagreeing	I can't accept the terms of your offer.	We aren't interested.
Offering to listen	What's your opinion of the matter?	I'd like to hear some more about that.
Agreeing to compromise	You raised a good point.	You're right about that.
Extending a negotiation	I think it's best we take another day to consider our options.	Let's think this over until Monday.

Lesson 8 – Taking a Position

Function	Formal	Informal
Stating a position	It is my opinion that raising the price is the best course of action.	I think you've got to change the logo.
Clarifying a statement	What I intended to say is that we need to find more funding.	I meant we need more time.
Providing evidence	Research proves a clear correlation between the two factors.	This study says we need a more direct sales method.
Showing understanding	Your view is correct, but try to understand my point of view.	You're right, but I think we need to do more.
Asking for feedback	I'm interested in hearing your thoughts on the matter.	Any thoughts?
Requesting more consideration	I think this matter needs further discussion.	Let's think this over.
Maintaining opinions	I believe strongly that this is the correct decision.	You can trust me on this.
Asking for agreement	Could you please try to consider what we are asking?	Please meet me halfway on this.
Closing a negotiation	With that, let's close our negotiation.	I think that's all.

Answer Key — Getting Started – Formal vs. Informal

Unit 3. Positive Interaction

Lesson 9 – Using Humor

Function	Formal	Informal
Easing tension	Please try to calm yourself.	Relax.
Offering encouragement	You will do better next time.	It's going to be fine.
Alleviating worry	There is nothing to worry about.	Don't stress yourself out.
Offering sympathy	I'm sincerely sorry to hear that.	That's too bad.
Accepting blame	It was completely my fault.	My mistake.
Warning	Please remember to proofread the report before you send it.	Don't come in late again.
Reassuring	Everything is going to be fine.	Stop worrying.
Downplaying a mistake	It's not that big of an issue.	No worries.
Congratulating	No one deserves this more than you.	You earned it!

Lesson 10 – Turning the Table

Function	Formal	Informal
Providing evidence	Please consider the results of the 2014 clinical trial.	Check out this marketing survey.
Asking for more information	Could you please elaborate on that statement?	Do you have any more info about that?
Disagreeing	I don't agree with your point.	I think that is wrong.
Highlighting an example	Consider the example of Apple's marketing strategy.	Disney is a great example of this.
Continuing an argument	Furthermore, increasing advertising would yield more revenue.	Also, this strategy would make us more money.
Stating an opinion	In my opinion, this is the best course of action.	I think we need a new sales strategy.
Offering a condition	I would happily agree if you increase your order by 3%.	Fine, if you sign the contract.
Conceding	Your argument has convinced me.	I can see your point.
Closing a meeting	Thank you for your time.	See you next time.

Lesson 11 – Invitations

Function	Formal	Informal
Setting a time	Would it be possible to meet at 6:00?	How about around 3:00?
Asking about food preferences	Do you enjoy Thai food?	How about Chinese?
Inquiring about schedules	Do you have anything planned for next Tuesday?	Any plans for tonight?
Accepting an invitation	I'd be delighted to join you.	Sounds like a plan.
Refusing an invitation	I'm sorry, but I have a schedule conflict.	Sorry, but I'm busy.
Asking for a suggestion	Could you recommend a good restaurant in the area?	What's good around here?
Offering a recommendation	You should try Golden Palace if you enjoy Chinese food.	The Mill Street Grill is the best.
Making a reservation	Do you have any tables available at 9:00 tonight?	Make me a reservation for 7.
Discussing dietary restrictions	Do you have any vegetarian options?	What's Kosher?

Lesson 12 – Maintaining Positive Relationships

Function	Formal	Informal
Complimenting appearance	Your new hair style really suits you.	Looking good today!
Making small talk	How was your weekend?	What's up?
Acknowledging an achievement	Your progress on the Italian project is admirable.	Great work on the Fairmont report.
Giving others credit	Mr. Johnson deserves the credit for this achievement.	It was all thanks to my team.
Accepting a compliment	Thank you, I really appreciate it.	Thanks for that.
Complimenting indirectly	What's your secret for dealing with difficult clients?	How do you get your hair to look so nice?
Offering a drink	Would you like some coffee while I'm up?	Want something to drink?
Offering assistance	Would you like some help with that?	Need a hand?
Wishing luck	I hope your presentation goes well.	Good luck!

BUSINESS BASICS 2

Unit 4. Cultural Diversity

Lesson 13 – Cultural Mistakes

Function	Formal	Informal
Introducing differences	My culture has a different view on the issue.	We do things a little differently.
Showing understanding	That tradition makes perfect sense.	Good point!
Demonstrating cultural values	My culture places a great deal of importance on punctuality.	Family is most important in our culture.
Showing respect for others' ideas	I value your input on this project.	That's a brilliant idea!
Talking about beliefs	I believe pursuing happiness comes first and foremost.	I think the number 13 is unlucky.
Explaining gestures	This gesture signifies appreciation.	Doing this with your hand means slow down.
Apologizing for misunderstanding	I'm sincerely sorry for the confusion.	I didn't mean it like that.
Explaining idioms	We use that expression to signify a meeting's end.	It just means that you did a great job.
Expressing surprise	That is such a shock!	Wow!

Lesson 14 – Cross-cultural Business Etiquette

Function	Formal	Informal
Asking to repeat information	Could you please repeat that number one more time?	I didn't get what you said.
Commenting on an error	I believe that is incorrect.	I don't think that is right.
Interrupting	Could I please add something?	Excuse me.
Offering an explanation	He might be late, because punctuality is not as important in Argentinean culture.	Maybe she said no because she doesn't eat pork.
Discussing etiquette	You should not cross your legs when we meet with the Saudi Arabians.	It's rude to say no if the host offers you a drink.
Politely disagreeing	You raise a good point, but I have to disagree.	I'm sorry, but that doesn't sound right.
Offering tips	Remember to be punctual for all meetings.	Don't forget to bring a present.
Demonstrating expertise	You can benefit from my experience.	I lived there for 4 years, so I can give you a few pointers.
Discussing protocol	When entering a business function, the most senior person present should always be given special treatment.	The meeting will be a working breakfast, so be prepared to wake up early.

Lesson 15 – Expatriate Employees

Function	Formal	Informal
Offering advice	Could I give you a little advice?	Need a pointer?
Asking about a schedule	When will you be departing?	When are you going?
Asking about a commitment	How long will you be working there?	What did you agree to?
Bringing up a concern	I'm just worried about culture shock.	What if I don't like it?
Making a suggestion	Have you considered taking a language class?	Try reading a guidebook.
Requesting information	Could you tell me what to expect in the negotiation?	Tell me more about the office culture.
Sharing new information	It was just announced that our office will be relocated to Bangkok.	Did you hear the good news?
Adding information	Additionally, you should avoid calling superiors by their first name.	Also, we need to submit the plan by Tuesday.
Expressing gratitude	Thank you for your kind advice.	Thanks for the tip.

Lesson 16 – Body Language Across Cultures

Function	Formal	Informal
Accepting an apology	No problem. I completely understand.	No worries.
Apologizing for misunderstanding	I'm sorry that I misunderstood.	Completely my misunderstanding.
Discussing cultural norms	In my country, we tend to value personal space more.	In Greece, it's normal for several people to speak at the same time.
Commenting on differences	In contrast to the U.S., initial meetings can often seem very formal.	That gesture means something very different in Italy.
Expressing discomfort	I'm sorry, but do you mind if I change chairs?	Is it okay if I open a window?
Offering advice	You should avoid exchanging business cards at social occasions.	Don't forget to bring a present.
Making an observation	I observed that people talk more animatedly.	It seems to me that punctuality is not as important.
Describing a gesture	To demonstrate that something is unsatisfactory put your thumb down.	A clenched fist is a sign of defiance or solidarity.
Asking for an explanation	What is the significance of doing that?	Why did you make that gesture?